BUDDY STALL'S

FRENCH QUARTER MONTAGE

BUDDY STALL'S

FRENCH QUARTER MONTAGE

By Gaspar J. "Buddy" Stall

HARLO PRINTING

Library of Congress Catalog Card Number: 92-73697

ISBN: 0-8187-0165-X

Printed by Harlo Printing Company,
50 Victor, Detroit, Michigan 48203

Dedication:

The three most important things in life are:
a loving family,
good health, and
true friends.
I dedicate this book to my oldest and dearest friends,
Pete and Elaine Mouledous, and family.

Acknowledgements

Special thanks to Roxanne Ryan, Clyde Morrison, Lane Casteix, Wade and Yvette Ponthier, Julie Scott, Irvin Bergeron, Robert Alford, Carol and Jim Rohde, Marietta and Richard Herr, Joe d'Aquin, Judge Dick Garvey, Bob Krieger, Thomas M. Finney, as well as the following people: Collin Hamer and the entire staff of the Louisiana Division of the New Orleans Public Library, Pamela Arceneaux and the entire staff of the Historic New Orleans Collection.

Foreword

For almost 100 years the French Quarter was the heart and soul of Louisiana. Every colonial governor assigned to Louisiana lived within its boundaries. These men were responsible for governing one-third of the territory of the present-day United States. They were required to overcome all adversities from river flooding to Indian uprisings. They were given the unenviable task of building a city that was to be located below sea level — not an easy task. They were also given the job of building houses that would stand up to the hot, humid climate where 60 inches of rain fell annually. This was to be accomplished without a system of drainage. And they had to do all of this on the newest land of all of North America. The land upon which the French Quarter rests is approximately 5,000 years old.

Not only did they accomplish all that was given to them to do, they built a city that would ultimately be called by many "America's Most Interesting City". In the course of achieving that illustrious title, the citizens of the French Quarter gave the country many firsts, among which were the first permanent opera house, the first apartment buildings, the first American world champion of sports (chess), first millionaire playboy, and the first Mardi Gras parade with floats, flambeaux, and masked riders. Within its boundaries were the largest federal building, the second oldest U.S. Mint, the first teachers of female and black citizens and the first female pharmacist. Oliver Pollock, one of its citizens, was the largest single financial contributor to the American's fight for freedom. Even though the area occupied by the French Quarter is small, it produced the first movie theater, the first ballroom dancing, the first department store, and the first printed money in the United States which was produced by the Citizens' Bank on Toulouse Street. In the Cabildo is found the original death mask of Napoleon, one of many of the city's treasures that is on display there.

Because of the wealth it had achieved, the first plush hotel, "St. Louis", was built, costing $1.5 million in the early 1800s. The French Quarter gave us the cocktail, along with numerous mixed drinks such as the world famous Sazerac. In the area of food, the French Quarter is the home of Antoine's, the oldest continuously family-operated restaurant in the world.

Jackson Square was originally called Place d'Armes, that is "public parade ground". The square is the most historic piece of land in the French Quarter, throughout Louisiana, and possibly the entire United States. It was the gathering place for the early citizens. Today, people from all over the world come to soak up its charm. It was in this historic place that flags of three different nations flew in just 20 days — Spanish, French and finally American on December 20, 1803. Just as the French Quarter is unique, the first American flag raised in Louisiana was unique, for it had 15 stripes as well as 15 stars. Facing the square is the second oldest Catholic cathedral in North America, and next to the cathedral is the Cabildo (court house) where the longest court battle in United States history, lasting 65 years, got its start. On the other side of the Cathedral is the Presbytere (priests' house) that currently serves as a museum. One of the many items on display is the first successfully built military submarine in North America. As young people sometimes do when looking for excitement, two young boys loaded a cannon in front of the museum, never dreaming it would fire. They were left with their mouths wide open and their ear drums almost punctured when it did fire. The ball barely missed the statue of Andrew Jackson and struck a house across the river, knocking a lady from her bed. Thankfully, she was not injured. Today the cannon's barrel is filled with concrete.

Through the years many famous people have lived in the Quarter. Celebrities from around the world have visited it, most coming back not once but many times.

A walk down Royal Street to locals is like New Yorkers walking down Fifth Avenue. Europeans are amazed upon seeing the French Quarter for the first time. Some elderly Europeans stated in reference to the Quarter, "It is more European looking than many of the European cities because of the destruction caused by World War II."

A few examples of the uniqueness of the French Quarter are as follows: Citizens do not walk on sidewalks, they walk on banquettes. They don't give directions using the points of the compass, but with an ingenious system understood only by locals. They don't have heavy clothing, for the winters in the French Quarter are very short. Last year, it was on a Wednesday.

Like peanuts, whereby you can't eat just one, the French Quarter is the same once you pay her a visit. It will not be just once. It has a magnetic attraction that causes visitors to come back again and again. Who knows? With a little luck, one day you could have the good fortune of living within its boundaries.

CONTENTS

CHAPTER 1

DISCOVERY
AND EARLY YEARS

WHY IT IS WHERE IT IS

FRENCH QUARTER
WHY IT IS WHERE IT IS

Until the Louisiana Purchase in 1803, the area of New Orleans now known as the French Quarter was the City of New Orleans. The Indians did not think much of the area. They called it Chinchuba, which means "alligator", for they felt the

New Orleans—early years.

term was most descriptive of the area. All the low-lying swampy area had to offer was alligators, mosquitoes and snakes. Added to that unpleasant combination, when spring came and the northern snows melted, the river overflowed its banks and flooded the area. To top it all off, the place was unbearably hot and extremely humid in the summer. No doubt the Indians shook their heads in disbelief when they saw the white men building their homes in this God-forsaken area. The Indians'

chant for the day had to be "dumb-de-dum-dums". If the Indians were right in their appraisal of the location, why in God's name was this area selected for what was planned from the very beginning to be a major city?

As a historian, I searched for the answer to that puzzling question for almost 15 years before I found an answer that made sense to me. The simple reason for the location is as old as mankind; it is called, "economic greed".

The following information will help to understand the reason for selecting the ungodly location we now call New Orleans. Although Louisiana was discovered in 1682 and named for Louis XIV, not much was done for many years to occupy or utilize its potential; the first attempt was not made until 1772.

At that time, Antoine Crozat, the secretary of the royal treasury and a man of immense fortune, received a 15-year contract from France for exclusive trading rights to Louisiana. The project proved to be a total flop.

In the first quarter of the 18th century, the Duc d'Orleans was serving as Regent of France. The king was only five years old and too young to rule. At this time, France was having severe financial difficulties that had been escalating from the time of the reign of Louis XIV — the extravagant Sun King. Into the picture comes the unsavory character named John Law. Law was a most unusual Scotsman, for he believed that if you earned a dollar, spend it, for the next day you might not be around to enjoy it. Law made his living as a professional gambler. When odds were against him, he would simply move in with a wealthy lady whose husband was away on business. Law was educated and had a brilliant mathematical mind. Still cards and other games of chance got the better of him from time to time. During one of these periods, he was living with a woman whose husband had an extensive library. One of the books Law read was in reference to banking principles used by several different cultures that used paper money. A brilliant idea bolted into Law's brain. He did his homework and went throughout Europe trying to sell his banking-with-paper-money scheme. Everywhere he went, people laughed in his face, all except the Duc d'Orleans. Law knew the financial straits France was in and used that as leverage to sell his banking scheme. Law told the Duc of his plan of building a major city on the Mississippi River that would serve as an economic valve for North America. Since the area of 33 present-day states emptied into the Mississippi River and almost all commerce moved by water, the proposed city would serve as a main cog in the economic wheel of North America. The best part, Law pointed out, was it would not cost the French government one franc. The Duc became interested, asking for further details on what Law called the Mississippi Company. It was simply explained; those who invested in the company would buy shares with their gold and silver. In return, they would receive part of the profit from the venture. Law, seeing that the hook had been set, made his next move. He then played on the Duc's ego. The new city will be named in your honor; it will be called New Orleans. The Duc's ego was suitably inflated. He fully agreed with the name choice. Law was ready to play his trump card. He said he had taken the liberty of contacting perspective investors, and, almost to the person, they were ready to invest their gold and silver. Law told Duc that all he had to do was to give the word. Duc could think of no good reason why he should not and agreed to the scheme. Law was a super salesman. He already had a street map drawn of the proposed new city complete with appropriate street names. He laid the map on the table for the Duc to see. "Since you are the principal in this project and the city will be named in your honor, it is only fitting the widest street, and the only wide street in the French Quarter, will also be named in your honor. It will be called Orleans Street. It will be eight feet wider than all other streets to show how important you are." He then asked the Duc of his son's title, to which the Duc replied, "The Duc of Chartres." He continued, "A street will be named Chartres in his honor. Since the Bourbons have great wealth and have agreed to invest, a street named Bourbon is to be so named." With no separation of church and state, Law felt it best to pay tribute to the religious. To accomplish this he named the street that was located in front of the St. Louis Cathedral, Church Street. Law told the Duc that it would be good business to name a street for the women who would be investing. He asked what a feminine French name was and was told it was "Ann". Law went one step further and suggested it be called Saint Ann Street. This was a wise move, for more and more females were coming into wealth. It was not learned until the 20th century what was causing so many capable, bright, young French nobility to die young. It was from lead poison from eating out of lead plates. To please the masculine side, the French Christian name of "Peter" was given. It, too, was to be given a saintly twist. It was called Saint Peter. Law had an ulterior motive for naming the streets Saint Ann and Saint Peter, which will be forthcoming.

Law's scheme left no stone unturned. He had just one more hurdle to cross. Knowing the Duc's feelings for some members of the royal family, he asked the Duc to be seated. After he did, Law explained the success of the project would require a couple of investors that might not be thought highly of by the Duc. He cautioned the Duc that the decision must be made on sound business principles and not personal feelings. The Duc asked Law who he was referring to. Law replied, "Toulouse and Dumaine." The Duc jumped to his feet and said, "I will not have those bastards in my city." Law calmly stated that they occupied the important positions of minister of the navy and finance; therefore, it was imperative that they be included in the project to guarantee its success. With his silver tongue, Law calmed the Duc down. With the map in his hands, he pointed out to the Duc that the main street — eight feet wider than all other streets — was named Orleans in his honor. He then explained. To protect you from the bastards, St. Ann and St. Peter Streets will serve as buffers between you and the bastards. He went one step further and explained the bastards would also be sandwiched by St. Philip and St. Louis Streets on their other flank.

The deal was consummated, the city was founded, and the Mississippi Company as Law proposed flourished. The French engineers looked over the information at their disposal and proposed that the best location for the new city would be the present location of Baton Rouge. It was felt that this high, dry ground would be the ideal spot. The economic flaw in their thinking was as plain as the nose on one's face. The men who were responsible for the success of the project knew that the mouth of the Mississippi River was closed much of the time by sand bars. Also, the swift current of the river would take two, three or even four weeks to reach the site they proposed. The decision to put New Orleans at its location was based strictly on economics. The present-day French Quarter, adjacent to the river, is a short distance from Bayou St. John which leads to

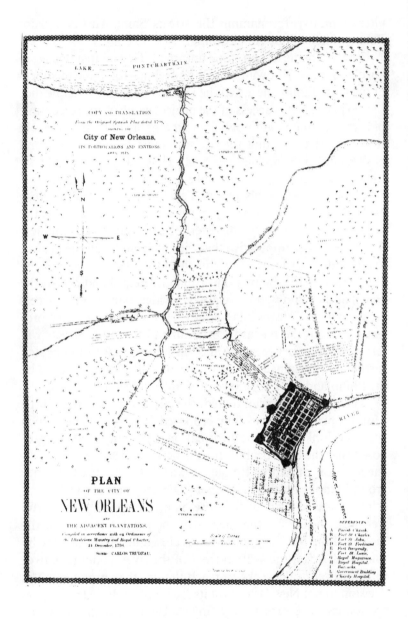

Lake Pontchartrain. From there, the water empties into the Chef Pass, to the Gulf of Mexico, and on to the world markets. In the eyes of John Law, flooding, mosquitoes, marshes and alligators could and would be overcome in the name of commerce. Or, as one historian put it, "New Orleans is located where it is simply because of one of man's oldest driving forces. It's called economic greed."

In his contract with the Duc d'Orleans, Law agreed that there would be a sufficient number of people to make the project go forward. Originally he fulfilled his contract. Those who were brought to the new land, frequently found the living conditions less than desirable and fled the scene. Law then set in motion a promotion throughout Europe, using a drawing of a cornucopia gushing with clear, fresh water from the Mississippi River. Gold and silver nuggets were all over the ground, waiting to be picked up. There was an unending supply of food that grew wild, as well as beautiful young Indian maidens running wild. Scores of those who saw the promotional poster came with great expectations. Upon arrival, they quickly realized that the promises shown in the promotional literature were false. The Indians' description was more accurate. Shortly after arriving, the settlers quickly went elsewhere. Finally, Law realized the dilemma he was in. To overcome the obstacle, he had laws passed in France that allowed anyone in jail to be set free provided they would come to Louisiana. Anyone out of work for a specified number of days was also sent to Louisiana. Prostitution being an illegal profession caused scores of loose females to be shipped to New Orleans.

In spite of all the problems, the Mississippi Company, or Company of the West as it was also called, was more successful than even optimistic John Law dreamed. Those members of the French nobility who invested their gold and silver were showered with a great return on their investment. Many purchased the finest thoroughbred racehorses to be found in all corners of the world. Some built large, luxurious estates. They were able to pamper themselves with whatever their dreams could conceive.

The Duc was pleased, to say the least. Prior to the venture he was always broke. Now he was a man of means. He bought a palace in Paris and a country place for his mistress. For her enjoyment he built a golden pagoda with one hundred monkeys. Whatever he wanted he got. Unfortunately he became a greedy man. He forced Law to print more and more paper script. It was only a matter of time before the bubble would burst, and finally it did.

John Law was the brilliant Scotsman who dreamed of a city that would conquer the commerce of a continent and did so. To many, he was considered the most fantastic promoter who ever lived. At the height of his success, he had a net worth of two million francs. Who knows how much more wealth had been acquired that was undisclosed?

Unfortunately, in spite of all the magnificent things that he achieved, John Law is remembered in history books not for being the brains for the establishment of New Orleans, but for being the father of inflation.

JOHN LAW

CHAPTER 2

PEOPLE

INTRODUCTION

FELICITÉ DE ST. MAXENT

JOHN J. AUDUBON

CATHERINE MARGUERITE MACNAMARA

PÉRE ANTOINE

WILLIAM RATCLIFFE IRBY

ANTONIO PEYCHAUD

NICHOLAS GIROD

JOHN B. SCHILLER

DR. FRANCESCO ANTOMMARCHI

DANIEL AND MYRA CLARK GAINES

BARONESS PONTALBA

INTRODUCTION

The best description of the multitudes of people who have lived in the French Quarter for the past 274 years would be to simply say, "My Cup, It Runneth Over." Even though small in size, the French Quarter has been home for a large number of innovative, highly successful, colorful people. Just a small smithering of those who fit the above description is as follows:

All colonial governors of Louisiana who governed Louisiana lived in the French Quarter. Governor Bienville, as a young boy, accompanied his brother Iberville on an expedition to discover the mouth of the Mississippi River. He is also credited with founding the City of New Orleans. Bienville served as the governor of Louisiana more years than any other three governors combined. He served faithfully on four different occasions (combined total of 32 years). He is also responsible, through the use of diplomacy, for quelling the first reported uprising in North America. It wasn't men carrying guns, but the good ladies of the French Quarter who protested by carrying pots and pans. They did so in revolt for not being able to cook properly because of lack of food products that they were familiar with. The local products were totally foreign to them. Bienville defused the uprising by appealing to the ladies' sense of fair play. He advised them that he realized something was wrong and had already sent his housekeeper, Madame Langois, to live with the Choctaw Indians on the north shore to learn how they properly prepared the local food products. He informed them that she had already been there three weeks and in another three weeks she would return to share her knowledge with them. Upon her return, she held the first home economic courses in North America. Madame Langois is credited with being the mother of Creole cooking. As already mentioned, she was the governor's housekeeper. Bienville did not bother to tell them that she was also his aunt. And we think of nepotism as being something new.

Besides the colonial governors, a number of American governors also lived in the French Quarter when the state capitol building was located in the old St. Louis Hotel on St. Louis Street (present site of Royal Orleans Hotel).

In 1743, the French Quarter changed drastically. In that year, Governor Pierre de Rigaud Amaquis de Vaudreuil-Cavagnal took over the reins of leadership. His background was saturated with lavish living and loads of elegant entertainment. His family had the necessary dollars to live the opulent life. Vaudreuil's father held the prestigious position of Governor of Canada. Because of his background, Vaudreuil, in a sense, became Louisiana's first royal governor. He is totally responsible for bringing society and elegance to an area that had been, up until his entrance, a backward town in the middle of a morass. The Grand Marquis was not about to stoop to the level that surrounded him. Instead he would lift the standards of living to his highly civilized level. This included installing the fine furnishings he was accustomed to. When all was in place, his dining room was illuminated by candlelight flickering from crystal chandeliers. When he dined he was served fancy, eye-appealing dishes on gold-rimmed china plates. When he drank, it was from silver goblets. He also brought musicians and other people of refinement with him. Under his tutorship, the first play staged in Louisiana was presented in the French Quarter. It was a tragedy called "The Indian Father". It was written by one of his highly educated, talented officers who knew who paid the bills. The hero in the play was none other than the Grand Marquis himself. Even though there is very little written information on the celebration of Carnival in the early years, what we do know is as follows: Besides introducing the theater to the French Quarter, a number of costumed, masked balls and soirees began when Vaudreuil was running the show. He served as governor for ten fun-filled, colorful years. When he was transferred, he threw a going-away party for himself that was every bit as exciting and dynamic as the people had come to expect. Of course, the party was also to introduce his successor, Louis Billouart Kerlerec. Even though it was a welcoming and bon voyage party, everyone there knew who the party was really for. The spectacular event was attended by 200 of the city's elite. They were entertained by chamber music and served champagne from three fountains that flowed continuously. Dinner consisted of food of every description that was as tasty as it was elegant in its presentation. Leading up to the finale was a colorful, loud and lengthy fireworks display that lasted three hours. For the finale, two pure white doves, each carrying sticks of fire, were released into the darkness.

Before leaving the political arena, let me mention a few words about French Quarter resident Judah P. Benjamin, who resided at 327 Bourbon Street. Although Benjamin was a short man, 5 feet 2 inches, he had no trouble climbing the mountain of success. He arrived in the city penniless in 1828, yet at age 30 was the owner and master of a sizable plantation. Also, he was elected to the U.S. Senate. When the Confederate States of America was born, he served faithfully and most capably in various capacities. He was Attorney General, Secretary of War, and Secretary of State during the heated conflict. He was called by the Yankees "The Evil Genius of the South". When the war ended, the federals put a price on his head, forcing him to leave the country. He made his way to England. Once there he had to start all over again. Benjamin was a highly competent and unique man. He was the first Jewish person in America to receive the honor of being nominated to the U.S. Supreme Court. President Millard Fillmore nominated him and was disappointed when Benjamin, because of personal reasons, was forced to decline.

Some other Quarter residents who made their indelible mark not only in New Orleans but the world were as follows: Paul Morphy became the first man from North America to be crowned world champion in sports. He was the world champion of chess. Paul literally rewrote the game. The way he rewrote it is the way it is played today. Another world-renowned resident was Louis M. Gottschalk, who lived on the fringe of the French Quarter on Rampart Street. Louis was a child prodigy, who mastered the piano when he was only six years old. He went on to become the first internationally known musician from North America. It was once predicted by the immortal Chopin that in his lifetime Louis M. Gottschalk would be the king of pianists. He was right. Gottschalk was a remarkable entertainer. If you had to compare him to anyone in reference to flamboyance, he was in the 1800s what Liberace became in the 1900s. In reference to his playing, he had no equal. He was also prolific in writing musical scores. Much of what he wrote is still played in concerts around the world. In the field of entertainment, French Quarter residents are proud that the first permanent opera company was located in the Quarter. The first ballroom dancing in America was on Orleans Avenue. The first movie theater was located on Canal Street. The first Mardi Gras ball, as we know it today, was born in the French Quarter. When the American Revolution was going on, Oliver Pollock, of Chartres Street, became the largest single contributor to the American cause for freedom. No other person or country contributed as much money as Pollock.

In the field of literature, my favorite writer of all time lived in the French Quarter. His name was Lafcadio Hearn. His writings are the most descriptive of anyone that I have ever had the pleasure of reading. If you have not read any of Hearn's work you are doing yourself a disservice. Other notable literary residents included Tennessee Williams, Dorothy Dix, Frances Parkinson Keyes and William Faulkner to mention just a few.

Today, the City of New Orleans has a reputation of being a fun-loving, easy-going, party town. It is one of the leading cities in the world where visitors come to enjoy themselves. The writers listed above, and scores of others who lived in the Quarter while they wrote, are greatly responsible for the popularity the Quarter has maintained for many years. Of course, we must not forget, the charm and mystique of the Quarter played its part in motivating and inspiring those who lived within her womb when they wrote about her.

Note: Dorothy Dix was the first nationally syndicated female writer in North America, as well as the highest-paid female writer in the world.

Stories of other notables who had residences in the French Quarter are as follows:

FELICITÉ de ST. MAXENT

Felicité de St. Maxent, who resided at 31 Rue de la Hospital, was the daughter of a wealthy Spanish merchant trader of the late 17th - early 18th century, Gilbert Antoine de St. Maxent. For services to his king, he was granted huge tracts of land in Louisiana. His shrewd business dealings made him even wealthier. In building his empire, he is best known in North America as co-founder of a fur trading post for New Orleans; today it is called St. Louis, Missouri. He was, without question, one of the best known and most talked about men in Louisiana in his day.

His daughter, Felicité, is surely not a household word in New Orleans today, but she was the most talked-about person in Louisiana in 1764. Some claimed she was even more so than her famous and powerful father. The reason: it was in that year she married the Spanish Governor of Louisiana, Bernard

⌐ FIRST LADY OF MEXICO ⌐

Galvez. When Galvez left his post in Louisiana, he was promoted to the lofty position of Viceroyalty of Mexico. This was, in terms of power, the position closest to the Spanish throne. When Galvez assumed his new position, Felicité became the first North American-born woman to become the first lady of a foreign country.

This was almost 200 years before another North American woman, named Grace Kelly, married Prince Rainier of Monaco.

Her story is proof that love and romance will always generate more interest with the general populace than money and power.

JOHN JAMES AUDUBON

John James Audubon, world famous ornithologist artist, was one of the many world-famous people who resided in the French Quarter, arriving in 1821.

Audubon's background was somewhat cloudy. It is a known fact that he was illegitimate. His father was a French sea captain, and his mother was a young woman from St. Dom-

John J. Audubon

ingue named Muguet. Audubon's granddaughter claimed he was the lost Dauphin, a member of the royal family. She claimed that after Louis XVI and Marie Antoinette were beheaded, the little prince, called Petit Fougere — meaning "Little Fern", was taken from Paris straight to Louisiana. Bernard de Marigny, a wealthy New Orleanian, claimed that Audubon was born at Fontainebleau, de Marigny's plantation on the north shore of Lake Pontchartrain (Mandeville). Records do show that Fontainebleau State Park, where de Marigny's plantation was located, was to be called "Birthplace of Audubon". But those involved in the project, upon learning of scandals regarding Audubon, dropped the idea. Marigny emphatically claimed that Audubon was born at Fontainebleau. He even went so far as to state that he was in the room at the time of the child's birth. Marigny also stated that when Audubon's mother, Muguet, died giving birth, the boy was taken to France and his fanciful name was changed to John.

As an adult, John returned to the United States, opening a store in Henderson, Kentucky, where he married Lucy Blackwell. They had two children. Audubon proved to be a poor storekeeper. In order to feed his family, he had to go into the woods to hunt. He became fascinated with the wild birds. When he shot them, he drew pictures of the birds before his family was allowed to eat them. Several years later, he had accumulated 1,000 drawings. Before he realized what was happening, a pack of rats shredded the drawings to make a nest. His reaction was simply to make better drawings. From Kentucky, he moved his family to Ohio. He learned there that instead of moving to various parts of the United States to find the birds he wished to draw, if he would go to the Louisiana delta and marshes, plus the inland forest where turkeys and other wild birds thrived, the birds, through migrating, would literally come to him. Audubon did not have enough money to buy passage on a steamboat but he came up with an ingenious idea. In exchange for passage, he told the steamboat owner that he would guarantee to feed the ship's passengers with game birds.

He was successful in making this arrangement and, along with his family, headed to New Orleans. After arrival it didn't take Audubon long to learn there was no work available for him in the city. He showed his paintings to the leading portrait painter in New Orleans. Sadly he was advised to give up the silly idea of becoming an artist, for he had no proper training and very little talent. To support his family, Audubon took a job tutoring children on plantations throughout Louisiana. His wife and children stayed in New Orleans, where Lucy worked at whatever job she could find. Life was not easy for the budding artist. After several years, Audubon returned to the French Quarter and opened his first studio at 706 Barracks Street. At this location, his work continued, but his family still faced near starvation.

Audubon became a man possessed. He moved to another studio at 505 Dauphine Street. In spite of the hard times, all the clouds hanging over him were not dark with despair. André Bienvenu Roman, a wealthy sugar plantation owner and Governor of Louisiana, who lived at 611 Royal Street, admired his work and encouraged him. Roman was honored to have this talented man as his dinner guest. He also officially subscribed to Audubon's mammoth volumes, thus keeping his dream, as well as his family, alive.

Audubon had the luxury of working in central Louisiana and described it as "next door to heaven." He also spent time in the delta where almost every conceivable species of birds landed at one time of the year or another. He found it was true, that Louisiana had more species of birds to observe and draw than anywhere else in the United States.

After many years, he felt his portfolio was ready to be shown and, hopefully, sold. If he thought things were bad before, he was in for the shock of his life. He became even more despondent when his work was rejected at every presentation that he made. No one in the United States, it seemed, was impressed or interested in his bird collection. Audubon, in spite of this, was a lucky man. His wife, Lucy, not only believed in him;

she saved enough money, by doing without necessities for herself, to enable him to book passage to Europe. When he arrived in London, he immediately contacted an engraver named Robert Havell. When he showed Havell his portfolio, Havell instantly saw the worth of Audubon's work and offered to finance its promotion. Havell believed it was so good he promised to make copper engravings for elephant folios. These engravings of Mr. Audubon's birds would be "on a scale of elegance never before attempted in England or any other country."

The rest of the story is history. "The Birds of America" was, in the opinion of many experts, one of the greatest works ever published and without question, the greatest collection of bird paintings by an artist. Even though he was told he lacked proper training and had no talent, he continued. While in the process, he and his family nearly starved to death. When the works were completed, he suffered the humiliating feeling of rejection in this country, not once, but every time he presented his work. Thankfully, he had not only the necessary talent, but also the determination and persistence to overcome all obstacles.

The Audubon Society today perpetuates his name with bird sanctuaries. There are so many, you would think he is some kind of scientific St. Francis. The fact is, at times he would shoot hundreds of birds and hang them on the walls of his one-room studio/home. Before he got around to painting them, most of the dead birds hanging on the walls began molting all over the place. Chances are if Audubon would try at this time to perform the feat he successfully accomplished at that time in history, he likely would be incarcerated for cruel and inhumane treatment of the subjects he painted and ultimately immortalized. The animal's rights people would have strung him up like he hung the birds he shot on his studio wall.

It is still uncertain as to whether Audubon was born in Louisiana on the Fontainebleau Plantation or in France as a member of the royal family. What we are certain of is he lived in the French Quarter and did become the king of bird artists.

JUST ANOTHER NEW ORLEANS PIGEON

In his journal, January 8, 1821, Audubon wrote the following, "I went to the review (celebrating the Battle of New Orleans) and will remember it and the 8th of January forever — my pocket was rifled of pocket book."

Audubon undoubtedly had a sense of humor (and little money), for he also entered in the journal:

"I think the knave who took it is now a good deal disappointed and probably wishes I had it."

No doubt, upon opening the purse, the thief said, "This guy is for the birds." Little did he know he was 100 percent correct.

**GOLDEN HAIR
WORTH MORE THAN A CASTLE**

On November 16, 1791, Catherine Marguerite Macnamara, daughter of an Irish count, married Jean Francois Merieult. Merieult operated the most successful import/export business in New Orleans. He was also an influential member of the illustrious Cabildo.

On April 25, 1792, Merieult purchased land on Royal Street (present address 529 Royal) for 1610 pesos. On this vacant piece of land, he built his home above his business offices. There he fathered three beautiful children, Catherine, Charles and

Euphrosine. His daughter, Catherine, was one of the most beautiful women in the city. Her long golden tresses were a sight to behold and the subject of many conversations. Catherine, as a young woman, accompanied her father to France on one of his business trips. While there, her beauty, and especially her golden tresses, attracted considerable attention. As in the Crescent City, numerous conversations revolved around her magnificent golden hair.

One lady, who was very impressed with Catherine's beautiful hair, described the color as that of "burnished gold".

About the same time Catherine and her father were in France, Napoleon Bonaparte was feverishly working to secure a political alliance with Turkey. Napoleon was advised that the Sultan of Turkey had searched far and wide for a human wig for his harem favorite. After an extensive search, the sultan was informed that the search had been unsuccessful.

Napoleon, looking for a wedge in his negotiations, began an all-out search of his own. He was pleased to learn from Josephine that her hairdresser had found such a head of hair on a lady named Catherine from New Orleans. Napoleon wasted no time; he immediately sent an emissary who made an offer of gold

to her father in return for her golden hair. The reply was a sharp "No." More gold was offered, with the same result. Several more attempts, with increased values of gold offered, resulted in the same negative reply. Finally, Napoleon made Merieult an offer he felt could not be refused. He had at his disposal a magnificent castle with beautifully manicured grounds and exquisite gardens. Napoleon was without question an expert in military strategy, but in matters of the value of a lady's hair he was wrong. Catherine would not part with her golden tresses for 100 barrels of gold or a beautiful castle.

You could say Napoleon had even less chance in capturing Catherine's hair than he did in conquering the world.

PÉRE ANTOINE
COLORFUL AND CONTROVERSIAL

Pére Antoine

For 40 years, Pére Antoine Sedella served as pastor of the Saint Louis Cathedral. It has been said that he was, without a close second, the most beloved and respected of all those who served in that holy position.

He came to New Orleans under peculiar, inauspicious and unpleasant circumstances. He was sent from Madrid as an emissary of the Holy Inquisition. Under the leadership of this good priest came the beginning and the end of the only attempt to introduce the Inquisition into the colony. It was in the year 1789 that the attempt was made.

Shortly after his arrival as emissary of the Inquisition, he met and paid his respects to Louisiana Governor Don Estevan Miro. After the formalities were over, the governor was told, not asked by, Pére Antoine, that his superiors demanded that the governor's troops be placed at the Inquisition's disposal whenever they were needed for arresting and punishing heretics. Governor Miro was most gracious during the strict demand for the use of his troops. He smiled, listened, and remained calm throughout the meeting. When it was over, he advised the Inquisition emissary that he would have his personal guards escort the good father to the convent where he would be residing to assure him of a safe journey. Antoine was more than pleased with the reception he had been given. As soon as he got back to his room, the holy man zealously began his secret preparations for the extinction of heresy in the City of New Orleans. Several nights later, shortly after he had gone to bed, he heard the heavy tramp of armed men marching along the corridor. Then came the bang of the musket butt against the door. Opening it the father saw a squad of Spanish soldiers headed by an officer in a colorful uniform. The officer and his men were stern faced. The good father was surprised, yet well pleased. He surmised, "They are here to assure me that they are at my service whenever needed." The priest informed the officers that he did not need them at this time, but would send for them when they were needed. He suggested that they retire with the blessing of the Almighty. "That is very fine," replied the officer grimly, "but the fact is we want you, and we want you to come with us now." The priest was in shock. For a moment he was speechless. He then collected his thoughts and threatened the soldiers with the vengeance of the Holy Inquisition. The officer was not intimidated. Pére Antoine was placed in the center of the squad and hurried to the levee where he was placed on a ship headed for Cadiz, Spain.

This was only the beginning of what was to be a long, stormy, roller-coaster ride of service to the church in New Orleans by

Pére Antoine under guard, run out of town.

Pére Antoine. Several years later, he returned. He had no further problems in his dealings with government officials. From this point on, his friction would be with ecclesiastical leaders.

During his tenure, he was once again deported by Bishop Cirillo for insubordination. Like a bad penny, the good priest, highly beloved by the faithful, but disliked by the religious leaders, came back again. When Archbishop Peñalder Cardeñas was transferred to Guatemala, the Louisiana diocese was left in the hands of Reverend Thomas Hasset and Reverend Patrick Walsh, both fiery, determined Irishmen. When Reverend Hasset died, Walsh was put in command. The personalities and tempers of Walsh and Antoine were incompatible. Shortly, Pére Antoine was informed that the everyday operations of the cathedral were to be taken away from him and placed in the hands of trustees, called "Marguilliers". To Revered Walsh's total dismay, the trustees elected Pére as pastor. Upon learning of this catastrophe, Reverend Walsh's face turned as red as his Irish hair. In retaliation, he designated the chapel of the Ursuline Convent as the parish church. When Bishop DuBourg arrived in New Orleans to take control of the archdiocese, he was so irked at what had transpired he suspended Pére Antoine once again. But again, his popularity with his

congregation, inspired them to come to his defense. They advised the bishop that they wanted their priest to serve them as he had always faithfully done. The parishioners searched through the town, but Pére Antoine was not to be found. Finally, some three days later, he was located on the outskirts of town, on the edge of a swamp, kneeling in prayer. It is believed that he was there from the time he was suspended from his duties. The parishioners carried him back into the church and placed him at the foot of the altar. They begged him to again say mass, christen babies, marry those who wished to be married, visit the sick, and aid the poor as only he could do. In response he told the crowd that he could do nothing until the bishop recalled him to duty. The fury of the group became great. They rushed through the streets toward the old Ursuline Convent where the bishop dwelled. The bishop was forewarned of what was transpiring and fled the city before they arrived. Many months elapsed before the bishop dared return. In short order he had to swallow his pride and reinstate the beloved Pére Antoine.

What made Pére Antoine such a popular religious person was his total dedication to his vows. It surely wasn't his looks. True, he had a grand old face. It was long, massive, and weather-beaten, and in the eye of an artist, it was beautiful. His snowy beard came down even to the hempen girdle at his waist. His habit was brown. His feet were always protected by wooden sandals. His holy look led to his being described as that of a medieval Saint Anthony. He lived in a humble dwelling that he built himself in the rear of the church on Royal Street. It was described as being not much more comfortable than a dog's house and as exposed to weather as a cow shed. He never refused when asked to visit the sick. The ragged purse that he wore around his waist was always available to those in need. His charity was greater than his modest income. He would go without so that those who needed his help were not turned away. His love of children and their love of him was bigger than life. When he walked the streets, children would come up to him, kneel in the mud and ask for his blessing. Of course, they knew he would always throw in a lagniappe in the form of a few small coins along with the blessing.

At age 81, the ever-faithful pastor passed away. Even in death he was a controversial figure. In his everyday simple attire, he was laid out in the cathedral. Thousands upon thousands of the faithful came to pay their last respects. In memory of his great service, newspapers suspended publication and courts closed. Even though not a common practice, all warehouses and businesses closed for the day of the funeral. The city council passed a resolution whereby all members pledged to wear crepe on the left arm for 30 days in his fond memory. The funeral procession began with the firing of a single cannon. The coffin was carried on the shoulders of four young men, surrounded by eight honorary pall bearers, all friends of the deceased. Following the coffin were soldiers of the Louisiana Legion, Catholic clergy, Governor of Louisiana, along with the Secretary of State, President and members of the Senate and the House of Representatives, judges of the Supreme Court, District Court, Foreign Councils, the mayor and clergy of the various denominations in the city.

Just as Francisco Antonio Ilde Fonso Moreno y Arze de Sadella, better known as Pére Antoine to his devoted followers, was highly controversial in life, he retained that status even in death. Among those in the funeral parade were large numbers of Masons of all branches. These men paid perhaps the greatest honor ever paid the priest's character. They ran the following glowing article in the newspaper to publicly express their feelings:

> "That venerable pastor, as tolerant as virtuous, as charitable as enlightened, is not only regretted by an immense population, but he deservedly enjoyed the esteem and regard of that numerous class of our community whose principles are founded upon faith, hope and charity — those sacred dogmas which Father Antoine preached as long as he lived. Masons remember that Father Antoine never refused to accompany to their last abode the mortal remains of our brothers, and that gratitude now requires that we, of all rites and degrees, should in our turn accompany him thither with all the respect and veneration he so well deserved."

PÉRE ANTOINE DATE PALM

Another of the controversies that continued after Pére Antoine's death concerned the tall date palm that grew in the priest's yard next to his humble abode. Articles in reference to the tree were written and run in numerous magazines and books. There were many stories of the tree, the most accepted was as follows:

As a young man, Pére Antoine and his young friend Emile

PÉRE ANTOINE'S DATE PALM

Jardain were planning to attend the seminary where their goals were to be ordained Capuchin priests. In their small town in Spain, a foreign woman from an unknown island in the Pacific — mysteriously appeared. Shortly after arriving, she died and left a 17-year-old daughter named Angelice. The young girl had a wild, strange, captivating beauty. The two young novitiates were both captivated by her, and both fell in love with her. In time, Emile and the girl eloped and returned to the Pacific island. Antoine, with a broken heart, returned to his religious studies. Many years later, knowing she was dying, and Emile having already passed away, Angelice sent her daughter to Pére Antoine, now serving God in New Orleans. Soon after her arrival, she became homesick for her island home where palm trees waved in the ocean breeze. She became ill. If it is possible to die of homesickness, it happened to her in this case. Pére Antoine buried the girl in the garden next to his home. Shortly after she was buried, a delicate green stem thrust through the earth just above the girl's burial place. In time, it grew into a tree, described by a botanist passing through town as a palm tree. The tree was a reminder of Angelice, the daughter of the one Antoine once loved. Through the years, the date palm grew taller and taller. He tended it with loving care. It grew to a great height and gracefully swayed back and forth when the wind blew. He refused to cut it down, for, as he said, it grew from the heart of little Angelice. To be sure that after his death the next land owner who purchased the property would not cut it down, he left in his will that if the tree was cut down the sale of the property would be forfeited, for the contract would be broken.

The tree was still growing and still a source of conversation 60 years after his death. As previously stated, there were many varieties of this story; one included his having fathered the young girl who was later buried in his yard on Royal Street. The exact year that the tree was cut down or died is not recorded. What we do know is that Pére died 183 years ago, and stories of his controversial, yet pious life, are still being written, read and hopefully enjoyed.

WILLIAM RATCLIFFE IRBY
MAN WITH A MISSION

William Ratcliffe Irby was a successful banker and the head of a large tobacco firm. He was also one of the city's many colorful philanthropists. He was tall, distinguished looking and rather handsome. His charity exceeded his pleasant demeanor by 100 fold.

William Ratcliffe Irby

In the 1920s, he noticed that the French Quarter was literally falling apart at the seams. Worst of all, no one seemed to care. Irby not only cared, he single-handedly began a resurgence of the Quarter. He surveyed the area and then began purchasing scores upon scores of historic buildings that had fallen into disrepair. One by one, he restored them to their original grandeur. Irby was not Catholic, but this did not deter his coming to the aid of the St. Louis Cathedral to the tune of $125,000. Through the years the cathedral had deteriorated alarmingly. The severe 1915 storm further weakened the structure. The foundation suffered severely when the city built its subsurface drainage system. Although it did what it was supposed to do, collect rain water to keep the city from flooding, it also lowered the city's water table. This caused the soil to dry out, thus creating a foundation problem. Conditions became so bad the church had to be closed to the public. Thanks to Irby, the necessary repairs were made and the cathedral was reopened. The $125,000 donation was made with the understanding that his identity be kept secret. It was not until after his death that it was revealed who the generous contributor was.

Another historic building that Irby purchased was located at 417 Royal Street. The building at one time housed Louisiana's first banking institution, Banque de la Louisianne. The bank's first president was Julian Poydras, who resided on the premises. He was also Louisiana's first poet. Another famous resident was Paul Morphy, North America's first world champion of chess. Today the building houses world-famous Brennan's Restaurant. Prior to that, it was a restaurant named Patio Royal.

After Irby purchased the building and restored it, he donated it to Tulane University.

William Ratcliffe Irby loved the French Quarter and did everything in his power to preserve its charm. When it deteriorated, he rebuilt much of it. When interest in its charm waned, he rejuvenated it. He was no doubt pleased and felt he had achieved all that he set out to do. One afternoon, Mr. Irby went to his club for a Turkish bath. Next he met with friends and socialized for several hours. Those in the party remarked afterwards how happy and content he seemed. He then went to one of his favorite restaurants, where he dined alone. From there he went to a mortuary to converse with Mr. Tharp, the funeral director. After Irby had made all necessary arrangements for his funeral, he asked Mr. Tharp if he might go up to the second floor to once again look at the casket he had selected and said he need not bother going up with him. A few minutes later a shot was heard coming from the second floor. The funeral director ran upstairs to find Mr. Irby in the casket. He had ended his life by firing his pistol into his temple.

Although Mr. Irby is gone, what he did to preserve the charm of the French Quarter remains with us today. Since there is no longer a cemetery in the French Quarter, Mr. Irby's final resting place is in the beautiful and equally historic place called Metairie Cemetery. Even though he was Jewish, it would have been a great Christian act of love if he would have been offered burial in the Cathedral for his great contributions.

ANTOINE PEYCHAUD

New Orleans has long been famous as one of the country's favorite watering holes. In fact, there were a number of drinking establishments in New Orleans long before there was a permanent church.

New Orleans prides itself in being the birthplace of the ever popular cocktail. It came about in the following way: There was a pharmacist named Antoine Peychaud whose pharmacy was located on the corner of Royal and St. Louis Streets. One evening after work, Peychaud and some of the members of his lodge held a meeting in the rear of his business. After the meeting, liquid refreshments were served. The pharmacist experimented by using the double-ended measuring device he used to mix prescriptions.

Coquetier

The piece of crockery used is called (in French) a "coquetier". The first cocktail was a brandy toddy with a dash of bitters and some secret Peychaud compounded to give it zest. The men were pleased with this new taste. They called it a "cocktail" in honor of the coquetier which was used to make the drink.

Cocktail

One of the city's most popular early cocktails was named for the highly respected Mayor Louis Philippe de Roffignac, who served from 1820-28. The Roffignac cocktail was made by pouring a jigger of cognac into a highball glass and adding a portion of raspberry or grenadine syrup, ice, soda and water.

It was said that anyone who could drink three of these potent cocktails in quick succession was also highly respected and could be mayor for the day.

NICHOLAS GIROD
CITY'S FIRST ELECTED MAYOR

In 1812, Louisiana became the eighteenth state of the United States. A very short time later, Orleanians were preparing to go to war against England. At the same time, they were also preparing for their very first political war. James Pitot, one of the earlier appointed mayors, ran against a highly successful, extremely proud Frenchman named Nicholas Girod. Girod was very shrewd. He convinced the voters (white male property owners only) that Pitot, as president of New Orleans Navigational Company, had a conflict of interest. Almost all commerce at that time in the city's history entered the city by way of Bayou St. John and the Carondelet canal. This water route was controlled by Pitot's company. It also proved to be an albatross around Pitot's neck. On election day, September 21, 1812, Girod won easily, 857 to 461.

When Girod was inaugurated, the ceremonies were held in French. The reason, Girod did not speak, read or understand the English language. When Girod took office, it was suggested that since he was now mayor of an American city he should learn to speak the English language. He, in return, suggested that since he was mayor let the people learn to speak French. In recent years, some people feel that some of our more recent mayors don't seem to understand the English language either.

MAYOR SWORN-IN IN FRENCH!

Someone jokingly said that when Girod bled he did so in red, white & blue, representing the tricolors of the French flag, not the American flag.

Nicholas Girod has the distinction of being not only the first elected mayor of New Orleans, he was also the first mayor to be re-elected.

As a staunch Frenchman and a great admirer of Napoleon, in the first quarter of 1821, Girod began construction of a house at 124 Chartres Street, at the corner of St. Louis. In the design was a circular room on the top level, with windows completely encircling the room. Its purpose was to serve as a lookout to survey the river in case the English came to capture Napoleon. As the house was being built, Girod purchased what was believed to be the fastest ship in the world. Her name was "Seraphine". She was outfitted and ready to go on a secret voyage to rescue Napoleon from St. Helena. The ship was to be captained by the famous Dominique You, one of Lafitte's capable lieutenants. Unfortunately, the Emperor died before the plot to rescue him could be carried out. The house built by Girod for Napoleon was called, what else, The Napoleon House. Even though the "Little Emperor" never made it to New Orleans, the structure has retained the title The Napoleon House. The building became the residence of Nicholas Girod. He died in the building on September 1, 1840, at 9:00 p.m. at the age of 90.

Girod's will proved that he was also a great philanthropist. He left $100,000 for construction of a building to care for "French" orphans residing in the State of Louisiana. Charity Hospital received $30,000 and orphan asylums in New Orleans $30,000. To five of his closest friends he left $150,000. The balance of the estate, which was quite vast, went to his family.

JOHN B. SCHILLER

During the steamboat era, the downriver corner of Canal and Royal Streets was called "Monkey Wrench Corner". The term was known to seamen all over the world as a meeting place for nautical men. It was where stories were swapped and unemployed sailors, called monkeys put the bite (loan) on those who were working.

The corner was equally famous in the 1800s for the famous Sazerac Cocktail which John B. Schiller invented in the rear of 116 Royal Street/13 Exchange Alley. The name of the establishment was Sazerac Coffee House after the brand of cognac he used. The brand was manufactured by Messrs. Sazerac de

Forge et fels of Limoges, France. Hence the cocktail was named Sazerac. Over the years it became the most-famous cocktail concocted in New Orleans. The fact that it originated here led to the legend it was named for a Creole family. This proved to be erroneous, as many fruitless genealogical researches have been made, with the results showing no such Louisiana family ever existed.

For those who have not had the pleasure of tasting a lip-licking, um-um good Sazerac cocktail, the ingredients are as follows:

> To properly mix a Sazerac requires two heavy bottomed 3.5 ounce bar glasses. One glass is filled with cracked ice and allowed to chill. In the second glass place a lump of sugar, using just enough water to moisten it. Next, crush with the bar spoon the saturated lump of sugar. Put a few drops of Peychauds bitters, a dash of Angostura, a jigger of rye whiskey, note: bourbon may do wonders for a julep, but it doesn't work for a real Sazerac. To the glass containing sugar, bitters and whiskey, several good sized lumps of ice must be added and stirred with a spoon. Do not use a shaker—use a spoon. In the first glass of ice, dash in one or two drops of absinthe, twirl the glass and shake out the absinthe. Enough will cling to the side of the glass to give the necessary flavor. Strain into the mixture. Twist a lemon peel over it, but do not drop the peel into the drink.

With this tasty appetizer some have said the drink was so good they did not get to the meal.

Today the location of the Sazerac Coffee House is occupied by Holiday Inn. The Sazerac name in blue and white letters is still visible on the sidewalk.

Dr. Francesco Antommarchi

DR. FRANCESCO ANTOMMARCHI

On May 5, 1821, on the Isle of St. Helena, Emperor Napoleon Bonaparte lay on his death bed. At his side was Dr. Francesco Antommarchi, Napoleon's friend and personal physician, who shared his exile. When Napoleon took his last breath, it was Dr. Antommarchi who pronounced him dead and closed his eyes for the last time. To preserve the moment for all eternity, Dr. Antommarchi made plans to construct a

Napoleon death mask.

mold for a death mask. Because of a severe storm, plaster necessary to make the mold was not immediately available. It was 40 hours after Napoleon's death before proper materials were obtained. This unfortunate delay, along with Napoleon's lingering and painful death that changed his appearance, were the main reasons for the death mask looking more like Caesar than the Emperor Napoleon.

In 1824, Dr. Antommarchi finally reached France with his cherished mold. He was able to obtain a royal mandate authorizing the French mint to make three bronze castings of Napoleon's death mask. The first of the three to be cast was brought to New Orleans by Dr. Antommarchi in November of 1834; the other two were placed in a museum and a hotel in Paris. The good doctor was received by the people of New Orleans with great enthusiasm. He was profoundly impressed by the generous sentiments of the populace. He was so moved, he donated the original casting of Napoleon's death mask to the grateful citizens of the City of New Orleans.

After a fitting parade, the mask was put on display in the illustrious Cabildo. It was appropriately placed in the same room where Louisiana, through Napoleon's maneuvering, was sold and later transferred to the United States on December 20, 1803. The mask of the dead exiled emperor remained at the

Napoleon's death mask in junk wagon.

Cabildo until 1852. At that time it was moved to the newly constructed City Hall on St. Charles Street. The War Between the States brought destruction as well as confusion. In 1866, after the war had ended, Mr. Adam Griffin, while walking on Canal Street, saw Napoleon's death mask being carried away in a junk wagon. He purchased the mask from the junk dealer, took it home and displayed it on his library table. Upon his death in 1890, it was given to Mrs. Robert Griffin, the widow of his son. She sold it to Captain William G. Raoul, President of the Mexican National Railroad, who brought it to his home in Atlanta, Georgia.

When New Orleans city officials finally found out where the mask was, they contacted Captain Raoul, who generously agreed to sell it back to the City of New Orleans for the price he paid plus interest. His only other request was that a fitting inscription of his act of love and compassion, but nothing about the sale price, be placed beside the relic. Mayor Martin Behrman willingly agreed to his terms. The death mask of Napoleon, like the man himself, was well travelled and controversial. After a 57 year absence it was once again placed in the Cabildo. During that period it went from Cabildo to City Hall to who knows where before being put on a junk wagon. From there to two private homes and then back to the Cabildo.

After 171 years Napoleon's death mask is still in the news. The most recent incident was the spectacular 1988 Cabildo fire. Thanks to the instant reaction of a brave New Orleans fire fighter, who disregarded his own safety and entered the burning building, the mask was saved one more time. When the Cabildo restoration is completed, this valuable piece of New Orleans history will once again be displayed for all to see. Right now it is once again in temporary quarters at the Presbytere.

DANIEL AND MYRA CLARK GAINES

Daniel Clark, in the early 1800s, was the most powerful political leader in Louisiana. His home was located at 823 Royal Street. He purchased it December 11, 1803, just nine days before Louisiana became an American territory. Daniel was as strong-willed and opinionated as he was rich and politically powerful. After William C.C. Claiborne became Governor of Louisiana, he and Clark had cross words. Claiborne made the mistake of challenging Daniel on the field of honor. Clark was

so sure he was right in the disagreement, when the two men stepped off the customary ten paces, Claiborne turned with one shoulder facing his opponent, lifted and aimed his pistol and was ready to fire. Clark in an act of defiance, simply turned and faced his opponent giving Claiborne a full target to shoot at. Clark stood there motionless and full of confidence, and told Claiborne to take his best shot. He further stated that he was so confident he was right he would give Claiborne a full motionless target. He would not aim or fire until after Claiborne had fired. Later, Clark was quoted as saying "Claiborne was as bad a shot as he was a politician — he missed by a mile''. Clark was an expert marksman and could have killed Claiborne had he wished to do so. Instead he shot his adversary in the thigh. Even though Claiborne was not wounded in a vital area, medical complications set in and almost ended his life. The governor was confined to bed for many months.

When Andrew Jackson arrived in New Orleans to make military arrangements to meet the mighty British army, his first stop after reviewing the battalion of uniformed companies of the New Orleans militia commanded by Major Louis d'Aquin, was at Daniel Clark's home on Royal Street. That in itself proved the power and influence that Clark wielded at the time.

Myra Clark Gaines was one of Daniel's children. She was also the only illegitimate child he reared. In time, Myra proved that she was more like her father than any of the other children. She learned well the lessons taught her by her father, especially the lesson of standing up for your rights when you feel you are being unfairly treated. When Daniel died, his vast wealth was to be equally divided among his living relatives as stipulated in his will. The only problem was that after his death the will mysteriously disappeared and was never located. The City of New Orleans contested the distribution of his estate, contending that his illegitimate daughter, Myra Clark Gaines, was not entitled to any of the inheritance. Myra, using the training she received from her father, went on the attack to defend her rights. She told the judge that her father had never deceived her. She, and all members of the family, were informed that she was a bastard. But, bastard or no bastard, she was his blood relative. Myra's defense was predicated on the term "Patrimony" (an estate inherited from one's father or ancestors). The trial began at the Cabildo. After 20-odd years, she was declared the winner. She was proud to have stuck by her guns as her father had taught her to do. It seemed the ordeal was finally over. But this was not the end. She was advised that she would have to take her case before the Louisiana Supreme Court. After so many years, it was believed she would throw in the towel. They were wrong. She not only fought her case in the Louisiana Supreme Court for over 20 more years, she won again. She was ecstatic about her victory. Again she was informed it was not over yet. She still had to take her patrimony case before the United States Supreme Court. Again, it was believed that after over 40 plus years she would hang up her gloves. Once more she fooled everyone. She not only went, but her case appeared before the United States Supreme Court 12 times until she was finally declared the winner of what had become a case with national interest. The patrimony case filed by Myra Clark Gaines, when completed, had generated over

40,000 pages of transcripts. It is to this date the longest court battle in United States history. She received not only the money she was entitled to, but also 65 years of interest.

Although Myra was the winner, what she gained more than anything was personal satisfaction. As anticipated, her legal fees ate up most of the monetary award she received.

MICAËLA, BARONESS DE PONTALBA

If a poll were taken to choose the most-colorful female to ever live in the French Quarter, the author's vote would be cast for Micaëla Leonarda Antonia Almonester y Roxas. Her equal-

Micaëla

ly famous and colorful father, Don Andres Almonester y Roxas, is covered in chapter five. When Don Andres' first wife died, it was not until 20 years later, at age 62, that he remarried. His choice was 29-year-old Louise de la Ronde. Since he had such good fortune with his first wife, who was about the same age as Louise, why change anything. Who knows, maybe it was love at first sight. Micaëla was born on November 6, 1795. Her father was then 71 years old, or, better put, 71 years young. What a man! On October 23, 1811, at age 16, Micaëla was married in the St. Louis Cathedral to her 20-year-old cousin Joseph Xavier Celestin Delfau de Pontalba. Because of the degree of consanguinity (descended from same ancestor) existing between the two, it was necessary to get a special dispensation from

the Vatican in Rome. With the vast fortunes of both families
this proved to be no problem. When it was obtained, the wedding date was set. On her marriage day, the child-bride openly
wept. Some said the poor thing was sad because her husband
was much prettier than she on her wedding day. The two great
family fortunes were now united. Together they created a small
empire. After being married, the newlyweds moved to France.
They lived in a magnificent chateau that is today the U.S. Em-
bassy. Unfortunately, the two fortunes did little to bring good
luck to the marriage. Aside from the enjoyment of her three
sons, Micaëla found no other satisfaction in her marriage. She
was totally unhappy with her wimp of a husband nicknamed
Tin Tin. She demanded a divorce, an almost unheard of thing
at the time. Upon learning of her intentions, her father-in-law
had a tissy. He was, to put it mildly, enraged. A divorce would
leave a black mark on his family name. He ordered Micaëla to
his Chateau Mt. L' Evecque to talk some sense into her. He
browbeat and chastised her for hours. She just let him rave on.
The more out of control he got, the calmer she became. She was
not intimidated in the least by his yelling and ravings. When his
verbal attack did little to sway her, he produced a pistol. He was
now totally out of control. In desperation, he aimed it at her
chest. Still she was not intimidated. She was surprised though
when he pulled the trigger and fired four rounds into her chest.
Her quick reaction in putting her hand over her chest saved her
life. Even though wounded as well as in shock, she quickly went
on the attack. While trying to wrestle the gun away from him, it
fired, striking him in the head. He fell back and slumped into a
stuffed chair. He was dead before his body settled into the soft
cushions. The servants, upon hearing the shots, broke into the
room. Micaëla was lying on the floor; her hand was mutilated,
and one finger was severed, but she was still alive. After she
recuperated from the wounds, she was as determined as ever to
sever herself and her children from the Pontalba family. When
the smoke finally cleared, she accelerated her crusade to get a
divorce. She had many contacts, including some in high posi-

tions in Rome. In time, by pulling the right strings, she did receive a divorce, as well as custody of her three children.

Note: Some writers claimed her father-in-law committed suicide. Others said Micaëla started that rumor.

Micaëla decided to move back to New Orleans, her native city. When she arrived, she was aghast at what she saw. It was blasphemous. She became as enraged with the situation as her former father-in-law was with her over the divorce. She found Creoles shopping in the American sector of the city. She could not believe her eyes when she saw the number of Creole families that were building in the suburbs and others considering doing the same. What could she do to stop the avalanche? She came up with what she considered a brilliant idea. She contacted James Gallier, the famous Irish architect. She told Gallier of property her father left her that faced both sides of Place d'Armes (today's Jackson Square). She then described a sensational housing and retail store project. It consisted of a combination of modern apartments with deluxe shops on the ground floor. Gallier was equally impressed and agreed to draw the plans for the two brick structures, each consisting of 16 houses. The cost of the two massive buildings was $604,000.00, a tidy sum in that day. The baroness was involved in every phase of the project from start to finish. She not only assisted in its design, she closely supervised the daily work. Every day of construction she put on men's trousers and climbed the ladders. Nothing was done without her hands-on supervision. Gallier couldn't take it and walked out, unpaid. No time was lost by Micaëla. Architect Henry Howard was hired to replace Gallier. Micaëla was so shrewd; after some time had passed she haggled with Howard over the price for which he agreed to do the work. The result, as usual, Micaëla got the better of him, and he received only a fraction of what they had originally agreed upon. At the persistence of the baroness, by daily inspections and constant driving of the work crews, both buildings were finished well ahead of schedule.

To put the finishing touch on the buildings, she designed the

Almonester and Pontalba grille work.

grille work on the balconies in the shapes of A's and P's to represent her maiden and married names, Almonester and Pontalba.

Once this project was out of the way, Micaëla moved to the next area of attack to bring the people back. This time the project was twofold. First, she wanted to rename the square between the two newly constructed buildings. Second, she wanted to dedicate a statue to Andrew Jackson. As a representative of the city in 1853, she had gone to Washington D.C. for the dedication of a statue of Andrew Jackson. When she saw it for the first time, she openly wept and vowed that one day the French Quarter would have one just like it. She went to work organizing the purchase and erection of a replica of the statue of Andrew Jackson in Washington D.C. Just as she had achieved everything else, the New Orleans statue of Andrew Jackson was dedicated in the center of the square, and the square was renamed Jackson Square in his honor.

The baroness was one tough, organized, dedicated lady. She was as fiery as her fire-red hair and twice as durable. When she set her sights on a project, she did not let up until it became a reality.

After all of her goals had been reached, she returned to Paris to live out the remainder of her years. When she died in 1874, age 80, she was again in the limelight in Paris. When they read her will she stipulated that she wished to be buried in the Pontalba family cemetery. Strange request since in life she could not tolerate her husband and divorced him. She could not satisfy, or grant her father-in-law his request by staying married to his son, and killed him. Yet there she lies close to both of them in eternal rest. Who knows, maybe she wanted to be close to them so she could continue to harass them in the next life.

One thing is for sure, she is closer to them now than she ever was when they were alive.

CHAPTER 3

MAJOR BUILDINGS

WHY FRENCH QUARTER MORE
SPANISH THAN FRENCH

BANK — HOTEL — ALLEY

CITY'S FIRST SKYSCRAPER

U.S. MINT

U.S. CUSTOM HOUSE

VITASCOPE HALL

919 ROYAL STREET

401-403-403 ROYAL STREET

TUNNEL IN FRENCH QUARTER

WHY
FRENCH QUARTER MORE SPANISH
THAN FRENCH

In 1788, New Orleans was not only prospering, but was considered the most regular, well-governed, small city in the western world. Good Friday was on March 21st of that year. Contrary to the Christian description of the day, it was not only a bad day for the city, but a disastrous one.

The military treasurer of the colony, Vincent José Nunez, lived on Chartres Street, one block from the Church of St. Louis. A fire broke out when the wind blew a lace curtain over a blessed candle on the private altar in his home. In a short time the entire house was ablaze. A strong south wind caused the fire to spread rapidly. The entire square was quickly engulfed in

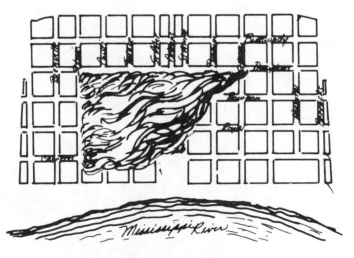

Good Friday Fire—1788.

flames. Explosions caused by unlawful storage of gun powder and ammunition in private homes caused the fire to leap across the narrow streets from one square of ground to another. By nightfall, 4/5 of the City of New Orleans (856 structures) lay in smoldering ashes.

When Pére Antoine, pastor of the Church of St. Louis, was advised of the fire and asked to ring the bell in the church tower, which also served as the fire bell, he stated that church regulations governing Good Friday services did not allow for the ringing of the bell on the anniversary of the day that Christ died.

Instead of the citizens running to put out the fire (no professional fire department at the time) upon hearing the fire bell, the flames danced from square to square. The only structure that was spared and is still standing today is the Ursuline Convent (completed in 1750). This was made possible by the quick action of Pére Antoine. He directed a bucket brigade of about a dozen men on the roof of the convent. They were able to keep the roof wet and extinguish any stray embers from the fire that landed thereon. The Church of St. Louis was not so lucky; it burned to the ground.

After the fire of 1788, the Spanish, who owned Louisiana at the time, rebuilt the city. They of course used their own Spanish style of architecture; hence, the French Quarter is more Spanish, architecturally, than French.

Ursuline Convent.

BANK — HOTEL — ALLEY

Prosperity in the 1830s brought great growth to the city of New Orleans, especially the French Quarter. Businessmen realized something more than small hotels and boarding houses were needed, as the city was enjoying a huge influx of visitors from all over the world. Architect J.N.B. de Pouilly was commissioned to build a stately columned, Greek revival bank building on Toulouse Street between Royal and Chartres Streets. When completed it was occupied by the Citizens' Bank.

St. Louis Hotel

In 1836, de Pouilly undertook another massive construction project. He was contracted to build the City Exchange Hotel, which was to be the first luxury hotel in America. When completed, it would occupy almost a complete square of ground bounded by Royal, Toulouse, Chartres, and St. Louis streets. It was to be first class all the way. Many of the materials were shipped from France. In 1837, construction of the building was halted because of a financial crisis. The promoters had to modify the size of the building in order to complete the project. Even though it was only half of the original plan, it was still magnificent.

The principal entrance was on St. Louis Street. There were also entrances on Royal and Chartres streets. The vestibule was 127 feet wide and 40 feet deep. The massive ballroom was located on the second level. The main feature of the building was the rotunda, a circular apartment with a high domed ceiling in the center of the building. Once opened, the hotel became the principal auction mart as well as the number one place for political meetings. Anything and everything of value, including crops, land, buildings, furniture and slaves were sold at this popular site. Many fancy balls and dinners were also held under its impressive, domed roof. The building was managed by

Slave Block

highly capable La Bourse de Maspero, who was assisted by a
Spaniard named Alvarez. The Spaniard operated the bar and
restaurant while Maspero took care of the rest. Alvarez proved
to be an innovator par excellence.

Wealthy men came to the hotel to buy and sell. In doing so
they spent numerous hours performing their chosen profession.

In 1838, Alvarez placed on the bar of the hotel the first free
lunch ever served in New Orleans, and probably in America as

well. When anyone bought a drink they were served soup, a
choice of meat, a helping of potatoes, plus meat pies and oyster
patties. In a short time, the innovation proved to be highly successful. In short order, all first class bars in New Orleans offered the same accommodations. The novel innovation then
spread to cities throughout the U.S.

Alvarez was so successful in this and other innovations, he
was selected to replace Maspero as manager when he left. In
1841, the hotel was engulfed in flames. By the time the fire was
extinguished the building was completely destroyed. No time
was wasted in rebuilding what has become a highly profitable
business. To save time, and no doubt stay with a winner, the

same identical plans were used. Like the phoenix rising from the ashes, the new building costing $1 million was reopened under the name St. Louis Hotel.

Just as manager Alvarez made great contributions, his successor James Hewlett, a well known sporting man of the period was destined to bring the hotel to even greater heights. Under his capable leadership the St. Louis Hotel became known for its splendor as well as its prosperity. The building became the center of the city's social life.

Among other things, Hewlett inaugurated a series of subscription balls, which became famous not only in New Orleans, but throughout the country. They were considered the pinnacle of elegance and magnificence. They were also without question the most expensive entertainment in the country.

Perhaps the most notable of these functions was the one given in honor of Henry Clay during the winter of 1842-43. Two hundred subscribers each paid $100 to be in that number. The ball and supper cost the enormous sum of $20,000.

It was also in this building's beautiful ballroom that for many years Mardi Gras dinners and balls were held.

BEGINNING OF THE END

When the Civil War began it marked the end of prosperity—but not history—for the elegant hotel. No longer were
grandiose dinners and beautiful Carnival balls the fare of the
day. And when the war ended, the city was placed under
Carpetbag rule. The building was purchased by the state of
Louisiana, and was used as the State Capitol building. The

State Capitol

ballroom sounds of old, the laughter of young couples and
soothing orchestral waltz music were now replaced by agitating
political voices of discontent. In the course of their misdeeds,
the corrupt legislature members passed taxes and laws that
brought tears to the locals and smiles only to the lawmakers.

After the Canal Street battle of September 14, 1874, called
the Battle of Liberty Place, between citizens aligned with the
White League and Kellogg's metropolitan police, the White
League took possession of the building and turned it into a for-
tress. After only two days they were ousted by Federal troops.

On January 4, 1875, when democratic members of the legislature attempted to take their seats at an initial meeting to organize for the session, Republican troops ejected them even though they were legally elected.

The Carpetbag government not only wrecked the economy of Louisiana, but left the building wrecked virtually beyond repair. The onetime elegant showcase was considered unfit and unsafe.

R.J. Rivers remodeled the structure and ran it for eight years before abandoning the project. You could say in a sense, the patient—meaning the hotel—was beyond help.

The last person to occupy the structure, even though the building was officially closed, was an elderly creole woman, whose only living relative, an older brother, died and left her to fend for herself. She lived in the condemned structure with her cat, horse, and a slew of bats. Although as loony as a bat, she was able to sustain life by charging clients 25 cents to take them on a tour of the once famous structure. She showed them the huge marble block where slaves were sold as well as the room where they were held until they were sold. She then showed with pride the ramshackle room that was once the elegant ballroom where the crème de la crème of New Orleans entertained themselves. Now the black and white marble floor was covered with dirt, plaster, pieces of broken brick, glass and other debris.

The final blows that brought the once structurally and financially strong hotel down were the 1914 bubonic plague followed by the devastation of the September 15, 1915, hurricane. The only course of action left to the owners was demolition.

The Old Citizens' Bank

THE GREAT PLAN

Still the project had been highly successful. Had it not been for the devastation to the economy brought on by the Civil War, who knows what the future of the hotel might have been.

The overall project was ingenious. The Citizens' Bank was organized to build the hotel. The bank faced Toulouse Street and the hotel faced St. Louis Street. The back door of the two structures met. Since almost everything of value was sold in the building, the alley, called Exchange Alley, leading from Canal Street to the front door was designed to make it easy for businessmen to make their way to the Exchange Hotel. The same architect who designed the hotel designed the alley. Entrepreneurs could secure whatever they wanted, needed or could make a profit from buying and reselling. The money received by the hotel was taken directly out the back door of the hotel into the back door of the bank. Pretty neat idea wouldn't you say?

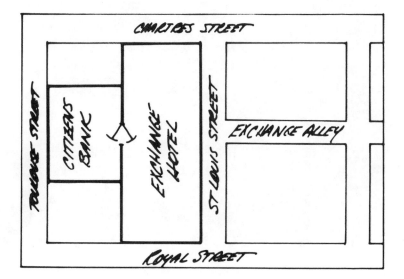

Bank and Hotel back to back.
Exchange Alley from Canal Street to front door of hotel.

EXCHANGE ALLEY

Besides serving as an easy route to the St. Louis Hotel, Exchange Alley became one of the most popular places in the French Quarter. It was here that many of the famous dueling masters set up their schools to teach the art of fencing. In fact, the entire length of the alley from Canal Street to the doors of the hotel was virtually filled with masters of the sword and rapier. Every afternoon and evening, those who walked the alley could hear the rasping of the swords, along with the sounds of the many spectators who could be found in every studio. It was a place where the young blue bloods practiced hour after hour to sharpen their skills. When the teachers and advanced students paired off, the amiable onlookers applauded or hissed as the case might be. As the duelling pairs moved around, grunting and sweating, the bystanders sipped coffee or one of the popular liquors.

Exchange Alley ran from Canal Street to St. Louis Street until 1910. In that year the entire block of houses surrounded by St. Louis, Royal, Chartres and Conti were torn down to make way for the civil courts building. When the civil court moved to its present location, the building was then occupied by the Louisiana Wildlife and Fisheries. Today the structure is virtually empty.

Some historians feel that the above mentioned French Quarter building is totally out of place architecturally. But keep in mind, for every misfortune to one person there is always good fortune to another and, in this case, many others. Because of the destruction of one complete square of French Quarter houses the red flag was raised alerting interested preservationists. Unless something was done to preserve what was left, soon the whole Quarter could disappear. That brought about the birth of the Vieux Carré Commission. Because of the commission, hundreds of buildings were restored, remodeled and renovated.

Today people from all over the world come to visit the French Quarter. To many it is considered more European than some cities in Europe.

CITY'S FIRST DOMED BUILDING

J.N.B. de Pouilly, architect for the City Exchange/St. Louis Hotel used a simple yet dignified external design. The interior was as elegant as the exterior was simple. Besides the massive vestibule and ballroom, the rotunda was a breathtaking sight to behold. The rotunda was 65 feet in diameter and reached a height of 88 feet above the floor. At the very top center, light from outside streamed into the massive room through a glass section designed for that purpose. De Pouilly used a simple solution to overcome a serious problem. In studying the weight of the dome, he felt that it would be much too heavy for the supporting walls, Tuscan columns and questionable foundation. He overcame this by using clay pots in the dome, forming a honeycomb and reducing the weight considerably.

FIRST PLUSH HOTEL IN THE UNITED STATES

The original hotel structure, built by de Pouilly at a cost of $1 million made New Orleans the pioneer city in America for providing housing for a large number of guests in comfort and luxury.

COST OF ROOM—1842

Comfort and luxury did not come cheap—not even in 1842. The St. Louis Hotel rate that year was $2.50 per day. The hotel also advertised that dinner for gentlemen would be served from 3:00 p.m. to 5:00 p.m. Ladies would be served after the gentlemen were finished. Women's lib was not in effect at that time.

OLD WITH THE NEW

Today the Royal Orleans occupies the location of the one time St. Louis Hotel. When constructing the present building, the same exterior design was used. In fact, on the corner of St. Louis and Chartres, the wall of the original Exchange Hotel was reused. Today, lettering is still legible and serves as a reminder of past glorious days of America's first plush hotel.

CITY'S FIRST SKYSCRAPER

For many years the bulky four-story brick building on the corner of Royal and St. Louis Streets was called by many who knew the old Quarter, the area's most interesting building. To the vast majority it was and is still called the city's first

First Four-story Building

skyscraper. Over the years the building at 640 Royal Street has had three names — the same number of stories it possessed when built in 1811. The three names were Doctor Le Monnier's Home, The Skyscraper Building and Sieur George's House.

The following is how the three different names came to be: For almost 100 years it was the consensus of opinion of builders that the soft, oozy soil of the French Quarter could not and would not support a building over two stories high. When the French Quarter was virtually wiped out by the fires of March 21, 1788 and December 8, 1794, construction of new buildings was everywhere. Still the rule of thumb of not building over two stories was adhered to.

In 1806, Pedro Pedesclaux, owner of the property and one of the best known notaries in the city, decided to build a new home to replace his single-story structure. In building the new residence he took two big gambles. The first was in borrowing a sizeable amount of money in a scheme that did not work out. The second was building the tallest residential structure ever built in the Quarter. He began construction but, before completing it, was forced to sell because of financial difficulties.

The purchasers were a noted physician, Doctor Yves Le Monnier and prosperous druggist, Francois Grandchamps. Once the property was legally transferred to them, they wasted no time in hiring not one, but two highly respected engineers and two architects. They went about the work of completing the partly-constructed building post haste. They decided during construction to heighten the walls of the mezzanine, making it even taller. When completed it would be three stories high — the city's first skyscraper. Sightseers gawked as the building reached higher and higher during the five months of construction. People would stand at the base of the building and look up. No doubt some wondered if it would topple over as others predicted it would.

Before Dr. Le Monnier moved in, General Lacarrieré, the project's engineer and also General Jackson's principal engineer at the Battle of New Orleans, laid out a beautiful

Terrace roof garden.

garden on the terrace roof. The doctor made his residence on the second and third floors. He selected the corner oval room on the third floor as his study. He would gaze out the window and with great pride look at his monogram "YLM" on the wrought iron work. It was prominently displayed on all of the wrought iron. The building became known as the Dr. Le Monnier Building, others called it the city's first skyscraper.

In 1876, Bertrand Saloy bought the property. He had started in business buying and selling bottles and rags. Just as

Wrought-iron balcony with monogram of Dr. Yves LeMonnier

his fortune went up, so did the height of the building. Shortly after he purchased the structure he added a fourth floor. He also had a garden laid out on the terrace roof. Although Saloy owned and increased the height of the building, it was never called the Saloy Building.

The third and final name of the building was "Sieur George's House," Sieur George being a character in a story written by noted New Orleans author George Washington Cable. Cable started his career as a writer for the Picayune. Over the years he observed the local French Quarter scene and kept notes. He eventually wrote the story called "Sieur George" that was published by popular Scribner's magazine. It met with great acceptance by people from all over the United States. The "Sieur George" story led to numerous other stories being published by Scribner. The Creole character in the stories was, of course, named Sieur George. He lived in the French Quarter. Although the exact location was not specified in the story, those familiar with the area knew instantly that it was the building at 640 Royal Street. Because of this, the building became known as, the Sieur George Building.

After 181 years the building that started off with three stories has been called by three different names. Just as the height increased to four stories so did the popularity of the building because of George Washington Cable's stories. Contrary to the belief of those who lived in the Quarter in the early years, the building does not tilt to the left nor to the right. It stands erect even though it was built on soft, oozy soil that the vast majority of people did not believe would support a structure over two stories high.

As great as Cable's story "Sieur George" was, and in spite of Dr. Le Monnier's monogram being in the wrought iron in numerous places on the structure, the building's most popular name is still the city's first skyscraper.

U.S. MINT
UNIQUE COMING OUT PARTY
LED TO EARLY
RETIREMENT (PARTY)

The small plot of ground on the edge of the French Quarter surrounded by Esplanade, Barracks, Decatur and Chartres Streets has had its share of colorful history. At one time, this was the site of Fort St. Charles, one of five forts that surrounded the French Quarter.

When American troops marched to Chalmette to defend the city in the Battle of New Orleans, Andrew Jackson stood before the gates of the fort and reviewed his assorted troops as they marched to meet the red coats.

When the five forts around the French Quarter were torn down, the square of ground occupied by Fort St. Charles was made into a park. It was appropriately named Jackson Square in honor of Andrew Jackson, the savior of the city, who reviewed his troops from this spot the week prior to the famous battle.

In the early 1830s, the federal government, realizing the need of increasing its capacity to produce coins, started a search for a suitable location for a new mint. Edward Douglas White, tenth governor of Louisiana and a prominent member of the Whig Party, orchestrated an all-out push to pluck this federal plum from the political tree of prosperity for his state. White proved to be a mover and a shaker. When others said it was virtually impossible, he was successful. The second oldest U.S. Mint (and first to mint silver coins) was built on the edge of the French Quarter on the site of Fort St. Charles.

The facility started minting coins in 1836. Public officials, the general public was advised, were eager to show off the workings of the mint. By the thousands, American citizens far and wide accepted the invitation and rushed to visit this unique and what some called extraordinary institution. For all, it was the first time, to their amazement, they actually saw the process of making money by stamping it.

Citizens were happy with their government and its willingness to show how it satisfied the need of coins for commerce. The government officials were proud as peacocks of the flawless operations at the facility.

All was tranquil until bureaucrats in faraway Washington were informed of nocturnal festivities that had been held without their knowledge in the heavily guarded mint. What they learned to their disbelief and consternation came about as follows: Joe Kennedy was the capable fun-loving director of the mint. He was also a prominent figure in the city's social life. When his daughter was ready for her debut into society, he naturally wanted to do it in grandiose style. The only problem was that his ideas exceeded his financial capability. After some deliberation, he found the solution. In fact, his unique plan was sure to be more spectacular than all the other coming-out parties, for it had never been done before.

Kennedy's soiree was to become the talk of the debutante season. He mailed regal invitations to everyone who was anyone to a fancy-dress ball — at the U.S. Mint!

Fancy dress ball at the U.S. Mint.

The evening of the event was like a Hollywood spectacle. Because of its unique setting, scores and scores of people attended in glittering costumes. Besides dining and dancing, excited guests strolled on that memorable night through the spacious offices, committee rooms and counting chambers. "But never," one guest remembered, "beyond the touch of a gendarme . . . these precautions gave a rather regal air to the whole affair."

Although the governmental leaders did learn of the fancy dress ball at the mint, the general public outside of the Metropolitan New Orleans area was never informed of what was referred to as that "grandest and most unique entertainment".

Director Joe Kennedy, apparently acting instead of reacting to the inevitable reprimand, took early retirement. Thank goodness he didn't consider holding his retirement party in the mint.

Although 1909 was the last year coins were minted at this location, the story of the famous debutante coming-out party undoubtedly will live on for as long as man has romance in his heart.

U.S. CUSTOM HOUSE

When the Louisiana Purchase was signed, the U.S. received not only the land, but all buildings owned by the French government as well. When France controlled Louisiana they felt customs duties would inhibit the growth of the city and therefore did not build a custom house building. Even though France did not build a Custom House, there was a Custom House building that changed hands at the time of the transfer. The structure had been built by the Spanish when they owned Louisiana.

After the Louisiana Purchase, the U.S. government realized the Custom House structure was inadequate for the growing commerce of the port of New Orleans. In 1807, Benjamin Latrobe, the architect who was appointed by President Thomas Jefferson to complete the nation's capitol in Washington, was issued instructions to make the necessary design for a Custom House building for New Orleans. As directed, the modest building costing $20,000 was constructed. It was the first federal building to be erected in the new territory.

Present U.S. Custom House.

In 1835, the New Orleans Bee newspaper reported that the government was looking into securing from Congress necessary appropriations to build a larger Custom House with a new and splendid edifice suitable to the wealth of New Orleans. Besides, the Custom House building was dilapidated and totally inadequate to handle the increasing volume of trade the port was enjoying.

The seed had been planted and the necessary work to carry out the project was on its way. There were three distinct reasons why the structure took 46 years to be completed.

PROCRASTINATION

Wheels of government, we all know, move irritatingly slow. There was no exception to this rule in terms of the Custom House. From inception to completion of the project, 13 different men served as president of the United States. This necessitated 13 different cabinets and many other changes in personnel as each president turned over the reign of government to the next. During the 46 years, the building had numerous architects and superintendents. Design changes after work began were beaucoup. Without question, procrastination played its part in the excessive length of time it took to complete the project.

LITIGATION

When the site of the new building was being selected, the city of New Orleans was having its own governmental problems. The Creoles were still apprehensive about democracy and forced the city into dividing the city into three municipalities. Each had its own council and city hall, but with one mayor serving all three.

The Creole French Quarter was in the first municipality, the location of the proposed Custom House. They were not receptive to the United States' request for the square of ground bounded by Canal, Iberville (at that time Custom House Street), N. Peters (at that time Front Street) and Decatur. The fly in the ointment was over the fact the building was U.S. government property, but the land in question, as seen through the eyes of the Creoles, belonged to the city of New Orleans. The U.S. government disagreed saying that both the property and the building were U.S. government owned.

When constructed in 1807, the building faced the river. It was within a stone's throw of the river when completed. Over the years the river built up additional land (approximately three blocks) between the river and the levee. The French term for this buildup in land is called "batture". The city claimed ownership since it was adjacent to its property. The council of the first municipality offered the U.S. government the batture or a piece of land close to the U.S. Mint. The U.S. government rejected the offer. The municipality adopted a resolution to put the piece of land on the auction block. This, they felt, would force the U.S. government to make a move. It did so in issuing an injunction to prevent the sale.

All this time, no progress was being made for a much needed larger Custom House building. Finally, the first municipality, for unknown reasons, offered the parallelogram-shaped property for a new Custom House building. The U.S. government graciously accepted the offer in 1845.

With this obstacle out of the way the next battle was ready and that was selection of architect and design of the building. This also proved to be time consuming with many changes before construction finally began in 1848.

CONFRONTATION

On November 22, 1860, P.G.T. Beauregard, then superintendent of Custom House construction, was reassigned to the prestigious position of superintendent at West Point. When Louisiana withdrew from the Union and joined the Confederate States of America, General Beauregard resigned and took the position of general of the Army of Confederate States of America.

On April 12, 1861, at exactly 4:30 a.m., General Beauregard gave the command to fire the first cannon round on Fort Sumpter. This marked the start of the Civil War. It also put the quietus on all construction work on the partially completed building. To protect the work already completed, the building was topped with a temporary roof. Once the war began, the building was seized and occupied by Confederate troops, and used as a factory to manufacture gun carriages and shells for Confederate forces. When New Orleans fell to Union forces, the building was retaken and listed in federal archives as FP (Federal Prison) number six, housing at one time as many as 2,000 Confederate prisoners of war.

After the war ended, construction resumed, but at a snail's pace, taking another 17 years before it was finally completed. When it opened in 1881, the 99,000 square foot building was the largest federal building in the country. It had 32,000 square feet more space than the capitol in Washington D.C. The building was so large, it was designed to have its own steam operated railroad within the building to handle the delivery of goods.

One of the highlights of the building was the business room located on the second floor, considered the finest business room in the world. It measured 95 by 125 feet and had a 54-foot high ceiling supported by 15 Corinthian columns, 41 feet high and four feet in diameter. Each cost $15,000. The marble capitals at the top of the columns each cost $8,000.

The massive four story building, built of granite with outside walls four feet thick and inner walls measuring two feet, six inches, was a challenge to the engineers who designed it — especially the foundation. After extensive study it was determined that to support the structure, the outer walls would have a footing that would be eight feet deep and 15 feet across (the inner walls' dimensions were 10 feet across). When the depth of eight feet was reached, the ground was leveled with an instrument. Three-inch by 10-inch cypress planks were then laid crosswise to the bottom. On these planks 12-inch by 12-inch cypress tenders were laid lengthwise close together and then bolted. On top of these,

Business room.

12-inch by 12-inch tenders were laid lengthwise three feet apart from center to center, leaving two feet between these tenders. These, too, were bolted together. Upon this grill and over the center of it was laid concrete two feet in thickness, firmly ramm-ed into molds seven feet wide at the base, brought up perpen-dicular to the top of the tenders and then sloped one to one on the sides, reducing it to five feet on the surface. On top of the concrete, brickwork was laid. The step brickwork came up to ground level and measured four feet across, sufficient to receive the four-foot thick outer walls. The same procedure was used for the inner walls with appropriate dimensions. The engineers estimated the building would settle 30 inches. They were not very far off. In recent years the settlement was measured at three feet four inches. The remarkable thing is the building has settled perfectly level with no noticeable cracks in the walls.

Yes, the U.S. Custom House is testimony to man's ingenuity. When good men put their minds to accomplishing a task, what one man can dream of, others can accomplish if given the necessary funds. Not even procrastination, litigation or confron-tation can stand in their way forever.

Definition:

Customs: Administers the powers and duties vested in the secretary of the treasury pertaining to the importation and entry of merchandise into and the exporting of merchandise from the United States. Principal duties are the collection of duties, taxes and fees due on import merchandise as well as the prevention of smuggling and frauds from the Custom House revenue.

VITASCOPE HALL
FIRST MOVIE THEATER IN THE U.S.

New Orleans in its illustrious history has had the distinction of celebrating many firsts. In fact, jazz, the very first art form in North America, was born in New Orleans. Just as virtually everyone knows that New Orleans is the birthplace of jazz, very few people know that the first movie theater in North America also operated in New Orleans.

Actually, the first movie in New Orleans was shown on an outdoor screen on the lakefront, June 28, 1896, by Allen B. Blakemore, an electrical engineer for the New Orleans City and Lake Railroad. Blakemore reduced the five-hundred-volt current from the trolley line for his wonderful vitascope machine by way of a water rheostat.

JULY 26, 1896   FIRST PERMANENT MOVIE THEATER IN U.S.

On July 26, 1896, the first permanent home for showing movies in the United States was opened at 623 Canal Street, on the corner of Exchange Alley. The name of the theater was Vitascope Hall and the cost of admission was 10 cents. For an extra 10 cents, you could get a look into the booth where the man was operating the vitascope. If you really wanted to splurge, for another 10 cents, you could get a frame of discarded film. Some people said it was a fad that would soon pass.

The theater accommodated 400 people and had two shows per day. The first began at 10:00 a.m. and the second at 5:00 p.m. Movies in 1896 were not long movies like today. They were made up of little skits strung together very loosely. They usually consisted of a fight scene, a floozy doing a hoochy-coochy dance, slapstick comics, and possibly even an embrace ending with a long, lingering, sensual kiss.

Those skeptics who said it was a passing fancy were wrong, for many people actually went to both shows. As we know today, movies are more popular than ever, even though many of today's critics said the popularity of going to the movies would decline with the introduction of VCR's and cable T.V.

919 ROYAL STREET
"SAVIOR OF CITY SERVED WITH SUMMONS"

General Andrew Jackson came to New Orleans to make necessary plans to defend the city from British invaders. He was surprised when he found himself being verbally attacked by local forces, long before the British forces arrived. The Tennessee general was not looked upon favorably by the Creoles. The fact is, many of them feared what he might do. When it was learned that the highly trained, armed-to-the-teeth British army, numbering over 5,000, would be going against a rag-tag, ill-equipped, untrained army of part-time soldiers they really became concerned. Even though the locals found Jackson to be dictatorial and arbitrary, this was not their greatest fear.

Rumors spread like wildfire after his arrival that he would adopt the "Russian" scorched-earth policy and destroy the city and surrounding area rather than let it fall into enemy hands. This naturally was of great concern to the wealthy city property owners. The bankers were also up in arms when they heard the rumor. Merchants with stores and warehouses filled with inventory joined the discontents. Added to that list were the plantation owners who lost sleep having nightmares about the possibility of their crops being burned and their warehouses and sugar mills being blown up by General Jackson, if he were forced to retreat.

Powerful political leaders began undermining Jackson's efforts to defend the city. Jackson made a counter-move that would ultimately lead to a legal battle shortly after the famous military battle of New Orleans.

Jackson felt he had no other recourse. He took drastic actions to overcome the drastic situation by placing New Orleans under martial law. The following military regulations were imposed on the city:

1. Every individual entering the city shall report himself to the Adjutant-General's office, and on failure shall be arrested and held for examination.
2. None shall be permitted to leave the city, or Bayou St.

John, without a passport from the General or his staff.

3. No vessel, boat or other craft shall leave the city or Bayou St. John without such passport, or that of the Commodore.

4. The lamps of the city shall be extinguished at nine o'clock, after which every person found in the streets, or out of his usual place of residence, without a pass or the countersign, shall be apprehended as a spy and held for examination.

When considering the dominant Latin temperament of the people, you can just imagine how martial law got their dander up.

Jackson's drastic actions generated opposition from members of the legislature, led by Chairman of the Ways and Means Committee, Philip Louaillier. The other thorn in Jackson's side was

Court House in which Jackson was Tried.

Judge Dominic Hall. Both men were volatile and highly vocal in their chastisement of the dictatorial general. Their statements were not only derogatory, but frequent. Both felt the imposition of martial law was a violation of their civil rights. They felt only Congress had the right to take such drastic actions.

Jackson struck back with the speed of a cobra. Using a counter-move considered by his adversaries as ruthless, he had Judge Hall, an Englishman by birth, and Philip Louaillier arrested and charged with aiding and abetting and exciting "mutiny". Jackson then went one step further and had Hall banished from the city.

The outcry was immediate. Jackson, it was charged, hated the French and never treated them with proper respect. In an attempt to prove this was an erroneous charge, he further fanned the flames of animosity by obtaining a release of Lafitte's pirates from jail. He further agreed that those in prison who enlisted in the American ranks and whose subsequent services met with his approval would be granted "a free and full pardon". Jackson figured that since many of them were Frenchman, this would appease his tormentors. In this case he was wrong.

History has proven Jackson's brilliant military ability. In spite of tremendous odds, he not only defeated the enemy, the victory was overwhelming.

Once victory was imminent, Jackson's unpopular martial law was abrogated. Judge Dominic Hall, Louaillier and others Jackson had sanctioned for their act of treason were at liberty again. Hall's first act was to serve the savior of the city with a summons (warrant for his arrest for contempt of court). Jackson was required to appear before Hall at court located at 919 Royal Street. Jackson, meticulously dressed in civilian clothes, appeared in court as ordered. The hall of judgement was crowded to suffocation by Jackson's admirers. Vindictive Judge Hall now had Jackson on his turf and he was ready to savor his moment of triumph. He found Jackson guilty of contempt of court and fined him $1,000.

Even though the indignant crowd violently opposed the judge's decision, Jackson, without protest, paid the fine in total silence and without a word of protest, left the courtroom. When Jackson entered his carriage, his faithful followers unhitched the horses. A number of them pulled while others pushed the carriage by hand to Maspero's Exchange. As they toasted the savior

of the city, money was collected to offset the $1,000 Jackson paid in fines. Jackson was truly moved. In a short speech he graciously thanked the men, but politely refused the money. He asked his supporters to always manifest their appreciation of the liberty for which they had so gallantly fought by a submission to law and order.

Jackson proved to be a winner at both the battle of New Orleans and the court house at 919 Royal Street. He won the respect and admiration of the masses at both locations by both his military and gentlemanly actions.

On February 14, 1844, 29 years after the famous battle and trial, the U.S. government vindicated Jackson of Hall's charges and forwarded him a check for $1,000.

On June 6, 1845, Andrew Jackson breathed his last breath. His last words were, "We shall meet." I wonder if he had Judge Hall in mind at the time.

401 - 403 and 417 ROYAL STREET
MANY FIRSTS
Louisiana's First Bank

When France and Spain owned Louisiana there were no banks in the territory. It wasn't long after the Louisiana Purchase that banking became a part of the everyday business operation in the city. In time, the corner of Royal and Conti became the banking intersection of the city. Three of the four corners of the intersection became banking institutions.

The city's first bank was appropriately named Banque de la Louisiane (Louisiana Bank). The institution was created on March 11, 1804 by Governor William C.C. Claiborne. It was located in the middle of the block at 417 Royal Street (presently Brennan's Restaurant).

The governor was censured by Albert Gallatin, the Treasury Secretary, who claimed that the bank began doing business without consulting the Federal Treasury Department. Perhaps the main reason, however, was because it was formed before the

U.S. Bank of Philadelphia could establish its branch in the new American possession.

Claiborne got out of the hotly-contested dispute when President Jefferson interceded on his behalf. With his assistance the bank was allowed to function as planned. The capital stock of $600,000 divided into 1,000 shares was subscribed and 15 directors elected.

The bank's first president was Julian Poydras one of the area's most progressive and prosperous citizens. Like many who started with little, he utilized his great sales ability. In his day, salesmen were called drummers (term handed down for centuries, because when a person came to town with something to sell he would beat a drum to get the attention of the people). Poydras, as president of the bank, purchased the building and land at 417 Royal Street on January 26, 1805. The property was previously an old mansion and residence of Don Jose Faurie, a wealthy French merchant. In order to serve banking needs, the building required some changes. The exterior changes worth

Plaque—Louisiana Bank

noticing were the wrought iron decorations on the balconies. On both the right and left side of the balcony railing can be seen the initials "L.B.". The monogram is enclosed in an octagon. In the center of the railing the Louisiana Bank initials are embossed on an iron plaque around which twine two snakes and a pair of cornucopias. This is a most unusual plaque for a banking institution. When looking very close you can see coins spewing from two horns of Amalthaea. If you think two snakes are unusual, spewing coins are even stranger for a bank.

Also on the exterior are the wrought iron supporting brackets under the central balcony. To architects and iron workers these are as interesting as the wrought iron balconies are to the multitudes who are compelled to look at them when passing the building.

In 1819 the banking operation expanded to the point where it was about to outgrow the building. It really didn't matter, for it was about to outlive its charted life at about the same time.

A new, larger structure along with the new name was needed. The bank took on the name, Louisiana State Bank since Louisiana was now the 18th state in the union. A new building was designed by Benjamin Henry Bonevel Latrobe, and constructed according to his plans. Unfortunately, he did not live to see the building completed. He died, as his son did before him, of yellow fever. When the Louisiana State Bank moved into the new structure in 1821, it had not only larger, more comfortable quarters, it also had one more initial in the monogram on the wrought iron balcony railing on the Royal Street facade "L.S.B."

Louisiana State Bank sold the property at 417 Royal to Martin Gordon, the socially prominent Clerk of the United States District Court. His residence became the center of French Quarter social activities. He was also active in politics and would defend his stance on any and all issues he supported. On occasions he would be found on the field of honor as a means of defending his beliefs. He killed one and seriously wounded numerous other opponents in this manner. He was not one to walk away from what he considered an injustice.

Monogram of the Louisiana State Bank on the balcony railing

Years before he purchased the building he was traveling through Tennessee and saw a man being attacked by two larger men. Without hesitation he went to the aid of the stranger who was taking a major beating. He drove the bullies off and helped the man to his feet. The tall, thin man, once on his feet, offered his hand to the stranger, saying "My name is Andrew Jackson — what's yours?"

In 1828, when Jackson visited New Orleans, he stayed as a guest in his old friend's home at 417 Royal. When "Old Hickory" became president, he did not forget the act of kindness years before. He appointed Gordon collector of the Port of New Orleans, a prize office at that time.

In 1848, when Martin fell on hard economic times, his home was seized and sold at a sheriff's auction to Judge Alonzo Morphy for $49,900. Although Alonzo Morphy's position as State Attorney General and a Louisiana Supreme Court Judge were great achievements, his greatest fame was in being the father of Paul Charles Morphy, the celebrated chess master. Young Paul was born June 27, 1837. Because June 27th was St. Paul's day, he was given the Christian name Paul. The house in which he was born was at 1113 Chartres Street; today it is listed as the Beauregard House.

Although Paul was born at 1113 Chartres, it was at 417 Royal

Paul Morphy

that he learned and through the years mastered the game of chess. Before he reached his teens he was able to defeat the best players of the New Orleans Chess, Checkers and Wisk Club, today called the Paul Morphy Chess Club. When young Paul received his law degree he was not of age to practice. He used the time before he could start work to travel throughout Europe and defeated all who faced him at chess. Howard Staunton, the leading English chess player was past his prime and refused to play the young master. Having defeated every famous player who challenged him, Morphy became the first world champion of sports from the United States.

The chess king died in 1884, at the age of 47, while still residing at the Royal Street mansion. Today the Paul Morphy chess club is the oldest chess club in North America.

In 1920, philanthropist William Ratcliffe Irby purchased the property. It was in deplorable condition. Once the building was refurbished inside and out he donated it to Tulane University. Since that time, two well known restaurants have occupied the premises — Patio Royal and world famous Brennan's Restaurant.

The people thus listed are just some who made history at this 417 Royal Street. It was the location of Louisiana's first bank as well as the location of the first Louisiana poet Julian Poydras and, of course, the home of the first world champion of sports, Paul Morphy. Besides these great men, Andrew Jackson, future president of the United States resided here when he visited the city.

413 ROYAL

This was the property of Dominique Roquette, who moved into the building in 1809, two years after it was built. As was the custom at the time, the balcony railing on the front of the building has his monogram "D.R." Mr. and Mrs. Roquette had

Dominque Roquette

four sons and one daughter. One of their sons, Adrien, became a beloved figure in the world of letters. He had a superb education, completing his studies in Paris. When he returned to his home, he sought the seclusion of the area north of Lake Pontchartrain. At Bayou Lacombe, he met and fell in love with a Choctaw Indian Chief's daughter. Her name was Oushola, meaning "Bird Singer". Adrien took the Indian name Chata-Ima meaning "like a Choctaw". Oushola was to sing no longer for her voice was silenced by death. Adrien was devastated by the loss and went into a deep depression. He could no longer stay on the northshore with the Indians he had come to love and respect for their simple way of life.

He returned to Paris where he buried his sorrow in law books. While in Paris he began writing volumes of poems, prose and other works. His efforts were enormously successful. He also received his law degree during this stay.

Even with all of this success he was still not happy or fulfilled with his life. He abruptly returned to his home. Upon arriving he decided to study for the religious life so he might become a missionary among the Choctaws. His religious studies completed, he was ordained to the priesthood in 1845. In doing so he was the first native-born to be ordained a Catholic priest. He spent the balance of his life spreading the word of God among the Choctaws north of Lake Pontchartrain, especially in the Bayou Lacombe area.

First Louisiana born priest.

TUNNEL IN FRENCH QUARTER
WAS THERE OR WASN'T THERE?

In both the 19th and 20th centuries, the story of a mysterious tunnel in the French Quarter has existed. Whether there was such a tunnel is still unconfirmed to the satisfaction of some historians. There is some written evidence that a tunnel did exist in the Quarter. This came about in an article that appeared in the Picayune newspaper on January 16, 1921. The heading of the one-half page article read:

BANKER'S TUNNEL OF OLD DAYS
UNCOVERED BY WORKING MEN
Secret Passageway Between Paul Morphy Place In Royal Street And House Back In Bourbon Under Most Famous Courtyard In The Vieux Carré.

The article both described where and possibly why the tunnel was built. As already described, Louisiana Bank, the city's first, was located at 417 Royal Street. As indicated in the headline of the newspaper article, it was later the home of Paul Morphy. In 1921, a little over 100 years after the Louisiana Bank operated, the building was occupied by Patio Royal Restaurant. During renovation of the building, evidence of the tunnel was uncovered by workmen both in the courtyard and inside the building.

The newspaper described the tunnel as, "large enough for a man of medium stature to stand upright and even for a slave loaded down with a great chest with which those bankers of long ago stored their piles of silver and gold. Its depth fell nine feet below the slab paved courtyard. The first glimpse into the dark, damp tunnel through the roof of which roots of the splendid old magnolia trees now towering in the courtyard have penetrated. The passageway brings those days to mind when through the courtyard echoed the voice of belles and beaus of Creoles, the laughter of pretty children, the strum of banjos in the slave quarters, sounds of music through the spacious drawing rooms which opened out upon the gallery in the enclosure in those days when the Rue Royal was still New Orleans fashionable center.''

The report further stated, "Glimpsing into the tunnel's crumbling passage brings to mind the reason for its secrecy—the days when pirate crews roamed at will, slaves were sold down river, and Louisiana changed hands so rapidly from nation to nation that save for the precious metals needed for exchange as far as the banks were concerned meant ever careful scrutiny.''

Apparently when the bank was in operation, the bank president was able to funnel money from within the bank under the courtyard to the backyard of the building on Bourbon Street. The newspaper article went on to state:

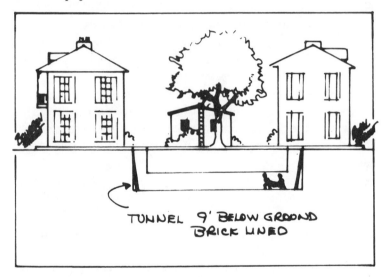

"But in the days when the old vault was installed and the walled tunnel dug, one even now can barely understand through the soggy, soft mud over which the Vieux Carré had been built the Louisiana State Bank boasted in vault and secret passageway, the greatest protection offered to its customers.''

The entrance to the tunnel was described as "Set deep in the wall in the queer old octagonal hall, a door beaten from iron by other slaves still guards the ancient vault wherein the ledgers of the institution reposed. Today while workmen under the direction of an architect are tearing down the cracked and mildewed plaster in that now dismantled wall, the old door guarding now the rubbish of a 100 tenement dwellers leaving still stands, its huge old knob and keyhole a vivid contrast to the great time locks and intricate bolts and sliding bars of the bank vaults of today. The tunnel leads direct under slabs of granite beneath high brick walls and outhouses into another courtyard in the Rue de Bourbon. There its exit is lost, filled with debris perhaps years ago. But its purpose still is clear, for so tradition hath it in that other live of two bankers." The 1921 article ended by stating, "The ancient tunnel, however, is still shrouded in mystery as its fate, but still, perhaps that also will be preserved."

The newspaper article was written by Hchmet Hassan. I believe you will agree he gave a vivid description of the tunnel and why he believed it was built. Also note the date of the article was not April 1st (April Fool's Day).

In the 1950s the building, once again, went through extensive repairs. The architect stated that although they did run across the doorway by the stairs described in the article, they were unsure of where it went and they found no further proof that a tunnel ever existed.

It seems that the controversy about the tunnel will continue, at least until there is some reason to dig nine feet deep in the courtyard between the Royal Street house that was once the Louisiana Bank and the building directly behind it on Bourbon Street.

The article, of course, is not conclusive enough to prove without a doubt that there was a tunnel. On the other hand, it sure goes a long way in keeping the controversy alive through the 20th century and likely well into the 21st.

CHAPTER 4

CHURCH

INTRODUCTION

DEFINITIONS

NAMED FOR LOUIS IX

FIRST CHURCH

SECOND CHURCH

GROWING PAINS AND EXPANSION

PRESENT STRUCTURE—
SECOND OR THIRD BUILDING?

SUISSE

CENTRAL TOWER

BISHOPS AND ARCHBISHOPS

HOW MANY BURIED?

LIST OF BURIALS 1796-1803

MORTAL REMAINS DURING RENOVATIONS
AND NEW CONSTRUCTION

FIRE TOWER

ONLY CHURCH FOR OVER 100 YEARS

CLOCKS

WORLDWIDE LEADERSHIP

INTRODUCTION

From the discovery of Louisiana on April 9, 1682, until the transfer of Louisiana to the United States on December 20, 1803, Louisiana was 100 percent Catholic. By law, there was no other religion allowed in Louisiana. France and Spain, both Catholic nations, administered to the religious needs of the people for 121 years.

Because there was no separation of church and state under France and Spain, the church, for all those years, was the focal point of almost all important activities. The Church of St. Louis, located across from Jackson Square, has had a full and colorful past. It has been administered by men from various parts of the world. It has also had its share of controversy.

The definitions of, and the stories of the St. Louis Church/ Cathedral/Metropolitan Cathedral and Minor Basilica are as follows:

DEFINITIONS

CHURCH/CATHEDRAL/
METROPOLITAN CATHEDRAL/
MINOR BASILICA

CHURCH:

A building for public, especially Christian, worship.

CATHEDRAL:

A church that contains a cathedra (a bishop's official throne) and is the principal church of a diocese.

Archbishop's Throne

METROPOLITAN CATHEDRAL:

Seat of an archbishop.
Double-barred archiepiscopal crosses on each of the smaller steeples of the St. Louis Cathedral signify that the church has the rank of metropolitan cathedral.

Double barred Archiepiscopal crosses.

Antoine Blanc was the fourth bishop of New Orleans and the first archbishop of the archdiocese, achieving this lofty position on February 16, 1851. Since the St. Louis Cathedral was being reconstructed at the time, he received the pallium (a cloak like the one worn by the pope) at St. Patrick's Church, which served as the Pro-Cathedral until reconstruction was completed.

Archbishop Antoine Blanc, in his 25 years of leadership, increased the number of churches in the archdiocese from 37 to 73. Church historian Roger Baudier remarked that Blanc's administration marked a turning point in the history of the Catholic Church in Louisiana. As he so aptly put it, Archbishop Blanc was "a prelate of sterling qualities, deep piety, great determination, high administrative ability, who possessed an unyielding insistence upon holding the right of the church, a genius for organizing and an incomparable builder of churches and schools."

Archbishop Blanc died June 20, 1860. On the 22nd, his remains were buried in the sanctuary of the St. Louis Cathedral.

MINOR BASILICA

In 1964, under the administration of Archbishop John Patrick Cody, the church was elevated to the status of a minor basilica. This was indeed an honor, for there are only 15 minor basilicas in the United States. The privileges of a minor basilica over a cathedral are:

Canopeum

Use of the canopeum — a large, ornate, partly-opened umbrella.

Use of a special bell encased in a replica of the papal coat of arms, with the picture of the patron of the church mounted atop a standard.

Spiritual privileges are bestowed from one of the five major basilicas, located either in Rome or Assisi, Italy. The New Orleans Basilica is affiliated with St. Mary Major Basilica in Rome. On certain feast days, the faithful who visit the minor basilica obtain the same indulgences as if they visited St. Mary Major Basilica in Rome.

For a period of 19 months, the church was called The Basilica of St. Louis King of France. On July 19, 1966, Archbishop Philip Hannan, at the request of Father Nicholas Tanaskoric, pastor of the church, restored the name St. Louis Cathedral. This change of name did not affect the church's status as a minor basilica.

CHURCH NAMED FOR
LOUIS IX

St. Louis, King of France

Louis IX, King of France, was born on April 25, 1215, in Poessy, France. He was only 11 years old when crowned king. Because of his young age, he literally trembled with fear at his coronation, even though he knew his mother would serve as Regent until his 21st birthday.

A well-rounded education played a large part of his early life. He became a master in Latin, an eloquent public speaker, and an accomplished writer. To round out his education, he was well-tutored in the art of war and the cunning of government.

Louis married at the age of 19 and fathered 11 children. His second daughter was married to Henry III, King of England.

There had never before been such a benevolent king in France. He ruled with kindness and understanding. He would not tolerate vulgar obscenities or thoughtless profanity. He always heard both sides of a dispute, even when his bishops were involved in the controversy.

The pious and righteous king was an endless supporter of the church, financially, religiously, as well as physically. He died in northern Africa defending the church while on a religious crusade against the Muslims on August 25, 1270. His last words on his death bed were, "Into thy hands I command my soul." His heart and bones were taken back to France and enshrined in the Abbey Church of Denise.

In 1277, just seven years after his death, he was canonized by Pope Boniface VIII. The St. Louis Cathedral, the second oldest cathedral in America, serves as a reminder of this champion of the church.

FIRST CHURCH

Although it was nine years before a permanent church was built, Christians living in New Orleans did have an opportunity to attend religious services. The first temporary place of wor-

1ˢᵗ TEMPORARY CHURCH

FIRST CHAPEL ERECTED ON THE SITE OF
ST. LOUIS CATHEDRAL, DESTROYED 9-11-1722

ship was located on St. Ann Street. It was a makeshift half-warehouse, half-chapel. On September 11, 1722, the first recorded hurricane struck New Orleans. The storm played

September 11, 1722, first recorded hurricane.

havoc with the area; every building in the new city was destroyed, including the building housing the temporary chapel. The winds were so strong three large vessels that lay in the Mississippi River were blown on shore.

The next temporary structure, located on Toulouse Street near the river, was described as "half of a wretched warehouse." It didn't last long; conditions were so deplorable the chapel was moved to a former tavern facing the river between St. Louis and Toulouse streets.

When Father Raphaël de Luxembourg, head of the Capuchin priests and first to administer to the religious needs of the people, arrived in New Orleans, he was unimpressed with the living conditions and the place where religious services were conducted. He immediately began a crusade to remedy the situation. He worked hard to have a new and proper church built.

Even though Governor Bienville, on March 29, 1721, used his loyal and valiant sword to trace the exact spot where the church was to be built, construction did not begin for several years. Father Raphaël did not give up; he continued to prod the officials. One more temporary location was used before the church became a reality. This one was in the military barracks across from present-day Jackson Square.

Finally, in 1724, construction of the first permanent church in New Orleans began; it was located on the exact spot designated by Bienville in 1721. Engineer-In-Chief Le Blonde de la Tour drew the plans, and French engineer Adrien de Pauger was responsible for construction. The structure was made of wood and brick, the first of its type in Louisiana. Both building materials were obtained locally. The construction style used was known as colombage. The process required stout timbers carefully cut and fitted together with mortise and tenon joints. All pieces were held together with wooden pegs. Pauger also had in his plans heavy timber buttresses on each side to brace the structure against hurricane winds. The building was so sturdy that during construction it was decided the buttresses were not needed. Before the structure was completed, de Pauger took ill and died. As requested in his will, his remains were buried within the unfinished building. After numerous delays, the new parish church was dedicated by Father Raphaël before Christmas 1727, and was named, as already described, for Louis IX. The structure was the most impressive building in the city. Over the door was a clock that rang only on the hour. A small belfry housed not one but two bells.

PARISH CHURCH OF ST. LOUIS 1727~1788

The permanent church was the pride of the community and the Capuchins. The first problem to surface once the church began services was not caused by faulty construction or the weather, but by the stormy faithful. As was customary at the time, armchairs were made available near the altar for the Governor and the Intendant. Two L-shaped pews were provided for members of the Superior Council and staff officers. All pews in the church were auctioned off to the highest bidders. This led to considerable rivalry amongst the parishioners, each wishing to obtain the most desirable seat. Just as the structure survived the damp, humid climate, the squabbling over pew space in time also passed.

In 1763, the harsh elements finally took their toll on the building. The holy structure had to be abandoned while necessary repairs were made. Once again, the people went to services in a temporary structure, this time in the king's warehouse on Dumaine Street. After many months, the building was finally repaired and reopened.

On March 21, 1788, the first permanent Church of St. Louis was delivered a devastating blow. The catastrophe has gone down in New Orleans history books labeled "The Good Friday Fire". The church survived the ravages of time, the elements and squabbling over pew space, but not the flames of 1788. The entire French Quarter was literally levelled to the ground. In all, 856 out of 880 structures lay in ashes, including the Church of St. Louis. This was the city's greatest catastrophe.

— FIRST PERMANENT CHURCH
3-21-1788 · FIRE

During the six decades that the church stood, there worshipped within its walls French Governors Perier, Bienville, and Kerlerec, and Spanish Governors Unzaga, Galvez, Miro and Manuel Gayoso.

For 61 Years, the first structure housing the Church of St. Louis was the center of community life in south Louisiana. Babies, be they lowly or highborn, free or slave, were baptized in the church. Couples were joined in holy matrimony. Sunday mass and all holy days of obligation were celebrated in the holy structure. Finally, through its doors, the mortal remains of the faithful were brought for burial rites of Holy Mother Church.

From the beginning of life to preparation for eternal life, and all times in between, the original Church of St. Louis served the faithful well.

SECOND PERMANENT CHURCH

After the Good Friday fire of 1788 burned itself out, it took nearly a year to clear the charred remains of the church. Once again, New Orleanians were without a permanent church building. Before another structure was completed, four different sites were used for religious services—the Chapel of the Ursuline, a hall in the government house on Decatur and Toulouse streets, Charity Hospital, and a building at the present site of the Cabildo.

Don Andrès Almonester y Roxas, a native of Andalusia, Spain, had powerful friends whose influence helped him to become one of the wealthiest, if not the wealthiest man in Louisiana. He was heavily involved in numerous commercial endeavors throughout the territory of Louisiana. Real estate and construction were just a few of the irons he had in the commercial fire. His ego equalled, and at times exceeded, his enormous capabilities. He was constantly working to achieve various awards and status symbols. He sought and received the rank of Captain and, later, Colonel of the Militia. He gained the prestigious title of Royal Notary for Louisiana. He was also appointed Junior Judge, Perpetual Commissioner and Royal Engineer, to name just a few of his numerous titles.

History proves that one man's misfortune is always another man's good fortune. The Good Friday fire was a misfortune for many people, but it turned out to be, in a sense, good fortune for title-hungry Almonester. Over the years, Almonester had performed a number of works of charity. He built a beautiful chapel for the Ursuline nuns at great expense. When Charity Hospital was severely damaged by a hurricane, he rebuilt it. To aid the unfortunate suffering with leprosy, he constructed a building for them on land he owned on the outer edge of the city. Some felt he had ulterior motives for his every action, including his charitable acts.

He became obsessed with receiving from the King of Spain the prestigious title of "Castile". The fire gave him yet another opportunity to gain the coveted title. Soon after the fire, he made plans to build a new church that would be much larger than the previous structure. It was to be designed by the highly-capable Don Gilberto Guillemard, a Frenchman in the military service of Spain. When completed, the church would be presented to his adopted city as a gift. If this didn't tilt the scales of the title of Castile in his favor, nothing would.

Although construction began in 1789, it took more than five years before the new church was completed. With great ceremony, the cornerstone was laid on February 14, 1789. Almonester felt that when word of his compassion and yet another act of charity got back to the king, the title would surely be soon in coming. He was as wrong as the 1788 fire was hot. Because of the lack of title action, work on the church progressed at a snail's pace. When Almonester learned that the members of the Cabildo had discussed the matter, work was speeded up. The speed of construction was up and down like the pulse of a man who ran full speed for a mile and then slowly walked the next mile.

The design of the church consisted of a rather low, flat-roofed building, flanked by bell-capped hexagonal towers that would house two church bells.

Before construction was completed and the church dedicated, two major events took place. In 1793, Louisiana and the Floridas became a new diocese. Luis Peñalder y Cárdenas was appointed first bishop of the new diocese with New Orleans being selected as his see city. The second event was very close to being another holocaust. On December 8, 1794, a second spectacular fire destroyed 212 buildings. Although the guard house next to the church was totally destroyed, by the grace of the Almighty, the almost-completed new church structure was spared.

Finally, on Christmas Eve, 1794, the much-awaited day for the religious, the laity and Almonester arrived. The blessed sacrament was transferred from the convent of the Ursuline to the newly-constructed church. At midnight mass, the structure was consecrated and dedicated a cathedral. It became the second-oldest cathedral in North America. For the great occasion, Almonester was seated in the special seat of honor. He was as proud as a peacock. As he looked over the faithful members of the congregation, they, no doubt, in turn looked at him. He was a very proud man. He had fulfilled his promise by turning over the church structure, costing him 98,980 pesos, ($100,000.00) to the proper parties. More importantly, he also finally received the long sought-after decoration which was presented to him by order of King Charles III.

Although he considered this his most-cherished award, it was not his last. On September 8, 1796, once again in the cathedral with a full complement of prominent citizens and high-ranking government and military leaders, the massive array of decorations pinned on his chest were enclosed in the order's great robe. Almonester, loving pomp and ceremony was delighted the robe he was presented for the occasion had a high mantle and long, flowing train. It was so long it required many attendants when he moved from one place to another.

This was the last of the numerous honors he was to receive. Someone jokingly said it may have been because there was no place left on his chest to pin another medal.

On April 25, 1798, at age 73, Almonester died. His remains were entombed in a crypt under the floor of the church he built.

As a reminder of this great man, a marble slab in the church tells of his generosity. In addition, the authorities of the illustrious Cabildo ordered a full-length portrait of Don Andrès Almonester y Roxas to be hung in City Hall.

Note:

Although Dom Luis Ignacio Maria de Peñalder y Cárdenas was appointed the first Bishop of the Archdiocese of Louisiana and the Floridas, he was not present for the dedication of the cathedral on Christmas Eve, 1794. When he received the appointment, he had numerous commitments in Havana, where he was stationed, and was unable to leave. He did not arrive in New Orleans until July, 1795.

The reason the church was dedicated without the bishop's presence is as follows: Church authorities decided the need was so great it would be better to dedicate the completed building rather than wait another six months. Had they waited for the bells to arrive to dedicate the church, they would have had a much longer wait. The bells did not arrive until 1804, at which time they were installed and christened St. Joseph and St. Anthony.

GROWING PAINS

In 1834, just 40 years after construction of the St. Louis Cathedral was completed, the congregation had outgrown the structure, and something needed to be done to remedy the situation. Church trustees consulted with renowned French architect J.N.B. de Pouilly. After study, he devised a plan that would add capacity. But, after further study he was not optimistic that sufficient seating could be achieved with this new plan. He went back to the drawing board and came up with yet another idea. The new concept included lengthening the church and adding galleries. Again, after reflecting on the situation, he still was not convinced this was the answer to the problem. Finally, instead of recommending enlarging the church, he proposed a most dramatic solution. His suggestion—move to a new location and build a new church. The location he had in mind was the land occupied by St. Louis Number One Cemetery on Basin Street. This new and unpopular plan not only upset the living, but would even displace the deceased, and, no doubt, displease the surviving loved ones. If this plan was approved, it would necessitate demolishing the cemetery and holding the remains of those entombed until a church could be built. The new structure would be designed to include "galleries" and a vault to bury the remains from the cemetery. This, de Pouilly felt, was a workable plan, for the bodies would remain in consecrated ground. Besides, the area he proposed had three squares of ground available. This was more than needed for the church and rectory and would allow for future expansion. When asked what would happen to the cathedral on Place d'Armes — his solution, like the cemetery problem, was simply to tear it down. His proposal of tearing the Cathedral down and digging the people up was about as popular with the trustees as having root canal work done without benefit of a pain killer. This led to a heated discussion that required a cooling-off period between de Pouilly and the trustees. It was such a knock down, drag out squabble it lasted 10 years. After the decade long cooling-off period ended, a less drastic approach, using the same church location, was proposed. It consisted of major reconstruction of the cathedral. The plan called for increasing both the length and height, plus adding an open, central steeple. The tall open steeple would be constructed of cypress. It would also have sufficient quantities of wrought iron to serve as ornamentation. In order to do what was proposed, additional land would have to be obtained. When this was accomplished, the next step was to find a contractor to do the proposed work. John Patrick Kirwan, a capable Irish builder, agreed to do the work. He signed the contract on March 12, 1849.

This date marked the beginning of what could be labeled the "Unholy Wars". De Pouilly's original specification, a part of the contract signed by Kirwan, spelled out that the two hexagonal towers and the lower part of the front wall supporting the towers, plus the lateral walls, were to remain. Once Kirwan got underway, the first fly in the ointment surfaced. Inspection showed the side walls would also have to be demolished. The New Orleans weekly Delta ran the following article on June 3, 1849:

> "The interior of this venerable structure, we perceive, is now entirely demolished by the architect who has undertaken the erection of the new building . . . We understand that a portion of the old side walls are to remain and will form part of the new building. This seems to us a great oversight on the part of the architect or the committee who may have the management of the affair in hands. The walls are cracked in several places and seem completely out of line. We trust that the intelligent and public spirited trustees of the Cathedral will, at once, see the propriety of demolishing the portion of the old and dilapidated walls yet standing so that the structure, when completed, instead of being a patch work affair, will be such an edifice as will reflect credit on its projectors and the great city of New Orleans."

Kirwan went back to the trustees. His $77,000 contract would have to be revised to rebuild the side walls. A supplementary contract for an additional $19,000 was agreed to on June 15, 1849.

The next problem that surfaced was the completion date. The contract signed by Kirwan called for completion by Christmas 1849. Christmas 1849 came and went and the structure was nowhere near completion. Looking back, the completion date not being met proved to be a minor problem compared to what happened on January 19, 1850. On that disastrous day, as workers went about their task, the uncompleted central tower began to sway back and forth like its foundation was made of Jello. The tower broke loose and, before it hit the ground, took

with it both the roof and side walls. The tower's fall caused an estimated $20,000 in damages. At this time, the finger pointing of blame began. Kirwan blamed de Pouilly who in turn blamed the contractor. It took months for experts to determine the actual cause of the mishap. The report stated Kirwan's work was below par in a number of areas. They pointed out that he failed to anchor the new brick work into the old front wall. Inferior bricks and poor mortar were used, plus the mortar was not given sufficient time to harden before additional work was done. De Pouilly added fuel to the fire by stating that Kirwan did not protect his masonry from the weather. He further claimed when the inferior workmen put up the scaffolding they allowed it to touch the fresh masonry. Because of this, vibrations were set off when workers moved around, causing weakened masonry joints. The finger pointing and name calling came to an end only when the church trustees fired both Kirwan and de Pouilly. The decision was then made to hire another architect/builder and the trustees would handle the subcontract work themselves. With this new team, it appeared that the storm of controversy had passed. On November 9, 1850, a daily Picayune article stated:

"The downtown Cathedral is now rapidly approaching completion. The spires of the two corner towers on Chartres Street have been erected, and only require slating to finish them. The gangs of masons, lathers, plasterers and bricklayers are busily engaged in the pursuit of their various occupations in all the various divisions of the interior of the vast edifice.

"Now that the roof is on and the frame work for the grand arch is erected, the spectator, standing below, may acquire some idea of the grand and impressive effect the interior will produce when the building is finished. Even in its present rough and incomplete state, the loftiness and lightness of the main portion of the interior edifice are very striking to the eye of the beholder.

"Every precaution appears to have been taken to strengthen the walls. A great number of large iron bolts have been inserted; connecting timbers put up; stout and not inelegant buttresses of brick built against the side walls on the outside."

Although two years late in completion, on December 7, 1851, Archbishop Blanc, assisted by bishops from Natchez and

Mobile, blessed the new structure. Just as the bells had not arrived for the first church in time for the dedication, unfortunately the altars for the new structure had not arrived. The celebration date of December 7, 1851, dedicating the new building, was somewhat apropos. During construction when the central tower fell, contractor and architect fired shots of incompetence at each other. The dedication date coincided with the Feast of Saint Barbara, the patroness of artillery men.

December 7, 1851
St. Louis Cathedral

December 7, 1851, dedication ceremonies.

New Orleans, from the very beginning of its history, has had a passion for parades. This momentous occasion naturally warranted a parade. The solemn, yet colorful parade began at the Ursuline Convent. It was headed by troops in multicolored uniforms who kept step to martial music and the ruffle of drums. As the parade reached the St. Ann Street corner of the Place d'Armes, the bells of the cathedral rang out. Simultaneously a 21-gun salute from artillery units along the river began their deafening tribute. When this was completed, Archbishop Blanc and his entourage entered the new cathedral. It was "packed to suffocation proportions." As they walked down the long aisle, clouds of incense rose to the ceiling and the organ began its thunderous rendition of "Ecce Sacerdos Magnus". The celebration and dedication was not only beautiful but quite lengthy, lasting four hours.

PRESENT STRUCTURE
Second or Third Building?

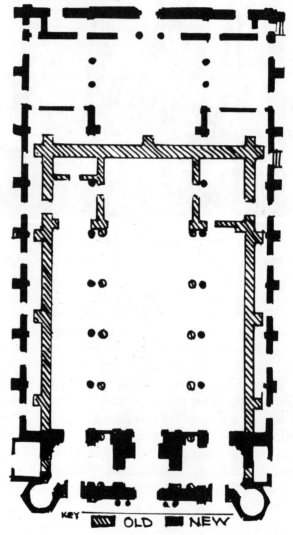

KEY ▨ OLD ▰ NEW

Over the years, there has been controversy whether the structure built by Don Almonester was the second, with improvements, or was actually the third structure.

In looking at the floor plan on page 140, it is apparent that there was very little of anything left of the structure built by Almonester. As is clearly seen in the plans, the old structure could literally fit inside the present structure since the latter is longer, higher and wider. True, when plans for renovation were made, the side and front walls were to remain. When the central tower fell, both side walls were destroyed. The only parts of the original structure that were incorporated into the new structure were the foundation of the main tower and the lower parts of the front walls under the hexagonal towers. It is very possible, but has never been confirmed, that even the front walls were either weakened and rebuilt, or totally destroyed when the central tower fell.

"SUISSE"

A European religious custom transported by the French to the Church of St. Louis in New Orleans was a character called "Suisse"—or, as some referred to him "beadle".

"SUISSE"

The Suisse was a fixture in the Church of St. Louis up until 1913. His duties included preceding the bishop and priest in all church processions, including weddings and funerals. He was, without a doubt, quite colorful in his regal uniform. It consisted of dark blue trousers, scarlet coat, and a gold-laced shoulder scarf decorated with the Papal Coat Of Arms; on his head, was a cocked hat trimmed with gold lace and a black plume; in his hand, he carried a large gilded spear.

Along with his ceremonial duties, his job was to seat the parishioners as they came into church and to keep order. While services were being conducted, he would walk with military pomp and ceremony up and down the aisles. When someone talked, he would vigorously bump his spear on the floor and turn and stare at the culprit, calling attention to the need for silence. As he peered at the violator, the daggers in his eyes were as attention getting as the six-foot spear in his hand. With these two weapons, very few people questioned his authority.

CENTRAL TOWER

When de Pouilly designed the structure, the central tower was open, airy and embellished with wrought iron ornamentations. Six years after completion, the spire was covered with weather-proof slate.

Because of the extreme height, the cross at the top of the steeple is deceiving in size. The cross measures 16 feet high and it is large enough for a six foot man to stand under the horizontal bar of the cross with plenty of head room above him.

Open steeple.

BISHOPS AND ARCHBISHOPS

The mortal remains of nine of the 13 deceased bishops and archbishops who have occupied the cathedra are buried in the hallowed grounds of the cathedral. Archbishop Hannan and Archbishop Schulte are still living.

HOW MANY BURIED?

From the earliest days of the Catholic Church, martyrs of the church—religious and prominent citizens both male and female—have been buried in the sanctuaries of churches. The St. Louis Cathedral holds the remains of untold numbers of religious as well as prominent men, women and children from various parts of the Archdiocese. The first person to be buried in the church (as already covered) was the French engineer of the first church, Adrien de Pauger, who died before the church was completed. The last to be buried was Archbishop Rummel in 1964. Although the total number is not known, listed below is a ten-year record showing names of 47 people who have been entombed in various parts of the church, including seven listed "not specified where."

PERSONS BURIED IN THE CHURCH
BETWEEN SEPTEMBER 13, 1793,
AND DECEMBER 24, 1803

1. The Reverend Father Francisco de Caldas, OFM Cap, former pastor at Natchitoches and later Chaplain of the Royal (Military) Hospital in New Orleans,
   buried in the Sanctuary of the Cathedral, September 13, 1793.

2. Maria Luisa Fernandez,
   buried at the foot of the altar of St. Francis in St. Louis Cathedral, October 4, 1795.

3. Eulalia Cruzat-Palao,
   buried at the foot of the altar of the Blessed Virgin Mary in St. Louis Cathedral, January 12, 1796.

4. Constancia de Reggio,
   buried in St. Louis Cathedral (*not specified where*), July 23, 1796.

5. Maria Bernody,
   buried in St. Louis Cathedral (*not specified where*), August 16, 1796.

6. The Very Reverend Alexandro de Carondelet, Canon of Cambrai Cathedral (brother of Governor de Carondelet), buried in the Sanctuary of St. Louis Cathedral, September 6, 1796.

7. Eulalia Aimé,
   buried in the chapel of St. Francis in St. Louis Cathedral, September 29, 1796.

8. Maneta or Ana Bernody,
   buried in St. Louis Cathedral (*not specified where*), July 19, 1797.

9. Francisco Morales y Guesnon,
   buried in the Chapel of St. Francis in St. Louis Cathedral, August 10, 1797.

10. The Reverend Father Jose de Villaprovedo, OFM Cap, Pastor of St. Bernard Parish,

buried in the Sanctuary of St. Louis Cathedral, September 20, 1797.

11. Male child Bosques,
    buried in St. Francis Chapel in St. Louis Cathedral, February 3, 1798.

12. Juana Maria Destrahan,
    buried in St. Louis Cathedral (*not specified where*), June 10, 1798.

13. Francisca Dellisle Dupart, wife of Antonio Pedro Marigny,
    buried in St. Louis Cathedral (*not specified where*), September 2, 1798.

14. Maria Antonia Marigni y Mandeville,
    buried in the Chapel of St. Francis in St. Louis Cathedral, April 29, 1799.

15. The Reverend Claudio Gerbois, Assistant pastor of this Cathedral and subsequently pastor of Pointe Coupèe,
    buried in the Sanctuary of St. Louis Cathedral, July 16, 1799.

16. Manuel Gayoso de Lemos y Sarmiento, Governor of the Louisiana Province,
    buried in St. Louis Cathedral (*not specified where*), July 19, 1799.

17. Maria Catalina Guesnon, wife of Don Juan Ventura Morales, Interim Administrator of the Province,
    buried at the foot of the altar of the Blessed Virgin Mary in St. Louis Cathedral, August 14, 1799.

18. Ana Dreux, wife of Francisco Bernoudy,
    buried in St. Louis Cathedral (*not specified where*), August 23, 1799.

19. Luis Alexandro Harang,
    buried in the Transept of St. Louis Cathedral, October 6, 1799.

20. Magdalena Carher, widow of Sanhago Beauregard,
    buried in the Transept of St. Louis Cathedral next to the chapel of the Blessed Virgin Mary, October 28, 1799.

21. Don Andrès Almonester y Roxas, remains transferred from

the cemetery to be buried at the foot of the altar of the Blessed Virgin Mary in St. Louis Cathedral, November 11, 1799.

22. Pedro de Marigny, Chivelier of the Order of St. Louis,
    buried in the Chapel of St. Francis in St. Louis Cathedral,
    May 15, 1800.

23. Male child Bosh, son of Bartoleme Bosh and Felicitè
    Fangui,
    buried at the step of the altar of St. Francis in St. Louis
    Cathedral, September 30, 1800.

24. Elena Paget, wife of Don Carlos de Grand-Pré, Governor
    of Baton Rouge,
    buried in the chapel of St. Francis in St. Louis Cathedral,
    December 21, 1800.

25. Reverend Father Luis de Quintanilla OFM Cap,
    buried in the Sanctuary (epistle side) of St. Louis
    Cathedral, February 1, 1801.

26. Reverend Father Mariano de Brunete, OFM Cap,
    buried on the epistle side of the main altar in St. Louis
    Cathedral, February 12, 1801.

27. Isavel Zara Moore, wife of Federico Zerben,
    buried in the first section of St. Louis Cathedral,
    September 6, 1801.

28. Magdelina Brazillier,
    buried in the Chapel of St. Francis in St. Louis Cathedral,
    September 10, 1801.

29. Luis Chauvin Beaulieu,
    buried in the Chapel of the Blessed Virgin Mary, in St.
    Louis Cathedral, October 11, 1801.

30. Carlota Volant, wife of Francisco Paschalis La Barre,
    buried before the gate to the Chapel of the Blessed Virgin
    Mary in St. Louis Cathedral, January 8, 1802.

31. Sara Juana Zerben,
    buried in the Nave alongside her mother in St. Louis
    Cathedral, February 6, 1802.

32. The Reverend Father Flavian de Besangon OFM Cap.,
    assistant pastor of the Cathedral,

buried in St. Louis Cathedral, February 9, 1802.

33. Andrea Antonia Almonester y Roxas,
    buried before the altar of the Blessed Virgin Mary in St. Louis Cathedral next to her father, April 9, 1802.

34. The Reverend Constantino MacKenna,
    buried in St. Louis Cathedral, gospel side, May 13, 1802.

35. Lorenzo Wiltz,
    buried in the Chapel of the Blessed Virgin Mary in St. Louis Cathedral, May 14, 1802.

36. Maria Juana Caron, widow of Jose Deville de Goutin,
    buried in the Chapel of the Blessed Virgin Mary in St. Louis Cathedral, June 25, 1802.

37. Maria DeVince, widow of Antonio Beinvenu,
    buried in the Chapel of the Blessed Virgin Mary, in St. Louis Cathedral, August 28, 1802.

38. Francisco Chauvin de Monplaisir,
    buried in the Chapel of St. Francis in St. Louis Cathedral, October 2, 1802.

39. Nicolas Domingo Berbois,
    buried in the Chapel of St. Francis, St. Louis Cathedral, November 2, 1802.

40. Manuel Serrano, General Assessor for the Province and voluntary Assessor for the diocese,
    buried in the Chapel of St. Francis in St. Louis Cathedral, November 14, 1802.

41. Francisco Raquet,
    buried in the Chapel of the Blessed Virgin Mary in St. Louis Cathedral, November 26, 1802.

42. Rosa Ramos,
    buried in the Chapel of the Blessed Virgin Mary, St. Louis Cathedral, November 28, 1802.

43. Juan Cheneau,
    buried in the Chapel of the Blessed Virgin Mary in the St. Louis Cathedral, December 6, 1802.

44. The Very Reverend Canon Francisco Perez-Guerrero, Canon of St. Louis Cathedral,

buried in the Sanctuary of the Cathedral, January 24, 1803.

45. Maria Magdalena LeCourt, wife of Santiage LeDuc,
    buried in front of the pulpit facing the Sanctuary Arch in
    St. Louis Cathedral, February 8, 1803.

46. Maria Genoveba La Source,
    buried in the Chapel of the Blessed Virgin Mary, St. Louis
    Cathedral, June 23, 1803.

47. Francisco Bichet,
    buried 30 feet from the gate of the Chapel of the Blessed
    Virgin Mary in St. Louis Cathedral, November 5, 1803.

LOUISIANA GOVERNOR BURIED IN CATHEDRAL

During the colonial period, 21 different French and Spanish governors or acting governors served in Louisiana. Of the 21, only one, Manuel Luis Gayoso de Lemos, is buried in Louisiana. He is one of the seven listed between 1793 and 1803 "not specified where".

Burial within church.

Gayoso was admirably fitted by temperament and training to execute his responsibilities. He was one of Spain's finest diplomats and was destined to rise to even greater heights. Unfortunately, his term of office was short, 1797-1799. His life was snuffed out at the tender age of 48 by the merciless yellow fever. During his tenure, Gayoso enjoyed a reputation rare among colonial officials. He never used his office for personal gain. One of the highlights during his governorship was the unique distinction of entertaining the future king of France, Louis Philippe, the Duc d'Orleans, (great-great grandson of Philippe d'Orleans, the regent of France, for whom New Orleans was named).

MORTAL REMAINS DURING RENOVATION
AND NEW CONSTRUCTION

What did the church do with the bodies buried in the church when a new structure was under construction or renovations of old structures were being made?

The remains were exhumed and moved to St. Louis Number One Cemetery. Once the new building or renovations were completed, the remains were returned to their original resting places.

Being done by humans, mistakes were no doubt made during the transferring of remains, leading to heading—"not specified where."

FIRE TOWER

Because the St. Louis Cathedral was the tallest structure in the French Quarter, for many years it was used as a lookout, or fire tower. Each night, a man was posted in the tower to watch over the city. The lookout tower was where the present-day clock mechanism is located. When he sighted a fire he would toll the bells. This would attract the attention of the people, who would look toward the church tower, where they would receive a lighted signal telling them in which direction the fire was located.

ONLY NEW ORLEANS CHURCH
FOR OVER 100 YEARS

The St. Louis Parish Church and its successor, the St. Louis Cathedral, was the only Catholic parish church in the city for over 100 years. It was not until 1833, 30 years after the Louisiana Purchase, that St. Patrick's Church for English- speaking citizens was put into service. Someone from the Irish Channel said it felt good to finally go to services where God spoke to them in English.

Note: In 1826, a mortuary chapel, now Our Lady of Guadalupe Church, was consecrated, but was used for burial services only for many years.

CLOCKS

The three church structures, as described, were different in architecture, but all had one thing in common, a large clock on the facade of the building. Although there is no specific reference to the clock installed in 1727, there is information on the one installed in the cathedral — not when it was dedicated in 1794, but when the central tower was added in 1819. The central tower was designed by Benjamin H.B. Latrobe, the noted architect of the U.S. Capitol and Benjamin Bouisson, a French engineer who once served in Napoleon's army. New Orleans clock maker Jean Delachaux was authorized by the trustees to secure a clock and bell to ring out the time. Delachaux purchased the clock and bell while in Paris. Delachaux, who was noted for keeping excellent records, had the following in his journal:

"When the new bell was ready to be put into the tower, I wrote him (Pére Antoine) a letter in Latin to apprise him of the circumstance, in order that, if the rites of the Church required any notice of it, he might avail himself of the occasion and do what he thought necessary. He thanked me, and I had the bell brought within the Church. After High Mass, he arranged a procession to the bell and regularly baptized her by the name of Victoire, the name embossed upon her by the founder."

After 173 years, the bell still rings out the hours. The following is the inscription on the bell in English:

"Brave Louisianians this bell whose name is Victory was cast in commemoration of the glorious 8 January 1815."

The same inscription is written in French.

The clock installed by Delachaux was removed in 1842. It was replaced by French clock maker Stanalas Fournier, who came to New Orleans to install clocks on prominent buildings. Fournier came up with a clever idea. With one single

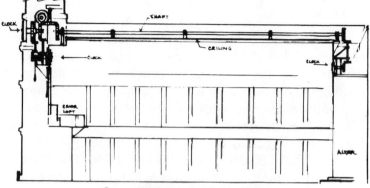

One mechanism operated three clocks.

mechanism he was able to operate three different clocks — one on the facade, one over the organ in the choir loft, and one on the rear wall of the church. The clock in the rear was operated by a shaft that ran the length of the church under the roof. Fournier came up with another ingenious idea for the principal clock on the front facade. It worked as planned, but came close to being a disaster. The plan called for the installation of a transparent glass dial. The dark hands and numerals were easy to read in the daylight. This was made possible by the black velvet drape behind the glass. For night time visibility, the area was illuminated by a gas light. All went well until the black velvet drape turned glowing red when it caught fire. Thankfully, it was extinguished in time. Had it gone any further, one could say they would have had the time of their lives putting it out.

The clock maker was without a doubt a real pro. Before the 20th century, the clock survived not only the fire, but a misdirected shot fired from a Yankee ship in salute of Admiral Farragut's arrival during the Civil War. In looking for a replacement dial, it is believed the dial of the Delachaux clock, installed in 1819, is the one they use to make repairs. In 1891, yet another disaster occurred. This time, lightning struck the clock. The clock's face still bears the marks of this mishap today. In this instance you could say that the clock took a licking,

TOOK A LICKING BUT KEPT ON TICKING.

but it keeps on ticking. And Timex thought they were the first to make that claim.

As the old saying goes, all good things must come to an end. The old clock mechanism that survived the test of time, fire, lightning and cannon shot was finally electrified in 1948.

CATHEDRAL
WORLDWIDE LEADERSHIP

In its 198 years of illustrious religious service to the community, the St. Louis Cathedral has been headed by only 15 bishops and archbishops. The average of 13-plus years per leader is rather remarkable considering some were advanced in years upon taking stewardship and served just a few years before retirement or death.

Just as the city was and is today made up of a polyglot of people, it is only fitting that nine of the 15 spiritual leaders were from various parts of the world. It was not until Archbishop John William Shaw, who took over in 1918, two hundred years after the city was founded, that an American born religious leader was in charge of the archdiocese.

As noted in the listings on the following pages, he was followed by Archbishop Joseph Francis Rummel, who was also foreign born.

Bishop Luis Ignacio Maria de Peñalver y Càrdenas   Cuba

Most Rev. Luis Penalver y Cardenas
First Bishop
1793-1801

Bishop Louis William Valentine Du Bourg   Saint-Dominge

Most Rev. Louis William DuBourg, S.S.
Second Bishop
1815-1826

Bishop Joseph Rosati   Italy
(Administered archdiocese affairs for four years, but was
not actually bishop of New Orleans Archdiocese.

Most Rev. Joseph Rosati, C.M.
Administrator of the Diocese
1826-1829

Bishop Leo Raymond de Neckére   Belgium
First bishop to be buried in the cathedral—1833.

Most Rev. Leo Raymond de Neckere, C.M.
Third Bishop
1829-1833

Archbishop Antoine Blanc   France
First archbishop to be buried in the cathedral.

Most Rev. Antoine Blanc
Fourth Bishop 1835-1850
First Archbishop 1850-1860

Archbishop Jean Marie Odin   France

Most Rev. Jean Marie Odin, C.M.
Second Archbishop
1861-1870

Archbishop Napoleon Joseph Perché   France
Buried in the cathedral in 1884.

**Most Rev. Napoleon Joseph Perche
Third Archbishop
1870-1883**

Archbishop Francois Xavier Leray   France
Buried in France.

Most Rev. Francois Xavier Leray
Fourth Archbishop
1883-1887

Archbishop Francis Janssens   Holland
Buried in the cathedral in 1897.

Most Rev. Francis Janssens
Fifth Archbishop
1888-1897

Archbishop Placide Louis Chapelle   France
Buried in the cathedral in 1905.

Most Rev. Placide Louis Chapelle
Sixth Archbishop
1897-1905

Archbishop James Hubert Blenk   Bavaria
Buried in the cathedral in 1917 (because the cathedral was
under repairs at the time, burial services were held at St.
Joseph's church on Tulane Avenue).
Thirty thousand people made up the funeral cortege from
St. Joseph Church to the cathedral.

Most Rev. James Hubert Blenk, S.M.
Seventh Archbishop
1906-1917

Archbishop Joseph Francis Rummel   Germany
In 1964 he was the 8th and last Ordinary to be buried in the cathedral.

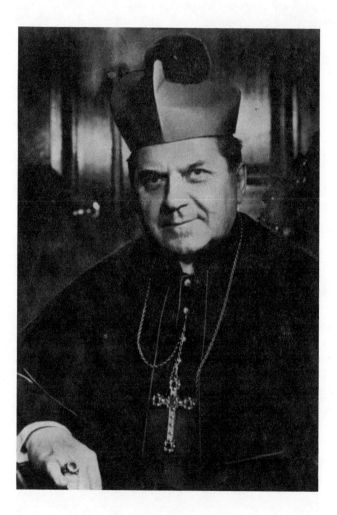

Most Rev. Joseph Francis Rummel
Ninth Archbishop
1935-1964

ONLY AMERICAN BORN

Archbishop John William Shaw   United States
First American-born religious leader to be buried in the
cathedral in 1934.

Most Rev. John William Shaw
Eighth Archbishop
1918-1934

CLOSE CHAPTER 4

The religious needs of the Catholic faithful have been administered admirably by the religious leaders of the Church of St. Louis. That is not to say all has gone as "smooth as silk," the contrary has been described in this chapter. Being human, both religious and laity with egos, varied personalities and points of view, at times led to confrontation.

In spite of this the church not only survived, but continues to thrive. After 274 years, the Catholic church is still the only denominational church to be found in the French Quarter.

In closing, this chapter that ends with burials in the cathedral, brings to mind the following story.

At the funeral of a New Orleans man, once the casket was lowered into the ground and the flowers placed on top of the grave, the priest and altar boys headed back to the limousine. As they walked back, the altar boys noticed an oriental family placing a bowl of rice at the front of a family tomb. Once this was done the family bowed in prayer. The altar boys seeing this, and no doubt being surprised, began laughing and whispering loudly to each other as to when might the person in the tomb come up to eat the rice. The senior member of the oriental family politely walked over to the young boys and softly replied, "As soon as the person you just buried comes up to smell the flowers." He then went back to praying in front of the little bowl of rice. The boys quietly walked away, hopefully having learned the lesson that we must all respect the traditions of others, no matter how strange they might seem to us.

CHAPTER 5

CARNIVAL AND MARDI GRAS

INTRODUCTION

CARNIVAL AND MARDI GRAS

The ever-popular celebration called Carnival began in Acadia, Greece, 5,000 years ago. The conquering Romans, liking what they saw, carried the celebration back to Rome. From there it spread to countries around the world. When the French explorers discovered Louisiana and decided to build a city there, the growing popularity of Carnival was brought to the new city.

EARLY CARNIVAL CELEBRATIONS

Transported with the celebration were the traditions such as masking, throwing of flour and sweetmeats (candy). The tradition of throwing to the crowds has been an integral part of the celebration from the very beginning. The day after Mardi Gras, writers described the French Quarter as looking as though it had snowed. The reason flour was thrown was that it made the streets and banquettes (sidewalks) look snow covered.

In the early years of New Orleans' history, muddy streets caused by frequent rains and no drainage system served as a deterrent to street parades. In fact, the celebration, as popular as it was, did not become a holiday until 1875, three years after Rex became a part of Mardi Gras. Up until that time, all celebrating was done after the working day ended. The largest public activities prior to parades were the Carnival and Mardi Gras balls. The refined French and Spanish Creoles had a passion for dancing. A French proverb states, ''The history of amusement is the history of civilization.'' A Spanish proverb claims that those who dance can never truly die. Lots of those early Creoles must have seemed to have eternal life, because in some years as many as 50 to 60 such balls were held during the Carnival season and on Mardi Gras. This was quite remarkable considering the population was just a fraction of what it is today. Admittance to the masquerade balls was open to the general public through the purchase of a ticket. After the Louisiana Purchase in 1803, a serious problem surfaced. New Orleans was now an American city with scores of hardworking, rowdy, rough river men moving into the area. The Creoles considered them unwanted intruders at their Carnival balls. They called them uncouth "alligator men". In just two seasons, the new element literally destroyed the once refined and enjoyable masked balls. The New Orleans City Council quickly and harshly reacted to defuse the highly volatile situation by issuing an ordinance that cancelled all Mardi Gras balls from 1805 through 1823. All masking on Mardi Gras was prohibited from 1806 through 1827. When the balls were allowed to resume, the Creoles decided to form private clubs for the sole purpose of eliminating the unwanted and undesirable Americans. The private clubs did accomplish everything they were designed to do. There were no further reports of disruption of the masquerade balls once they were restricted to members only.

In 1856, Carnival mayhem once again came to a boiling point. The ruckus was not at the private masked balls but in the streets. For some years prior to 1856, the mask of Mardi Gras was used to hide behind in order to do harm to one's enemies. New Orleans for a number of years was the destination of thousands of immigrants from Ireland. The new arrivals were on the lower economic rung and, therefore, were in direct competition with free black workers. As a result of the Irish immigration, at one time every fifth person in the city of New Orleans was directly from Ireland. The problem reached a climax in 1856 when brickbats were thrown in place of sweetmeats. Lime was thrown in place of flour. It was purposely thrown into the faces and eyes of the respective enemies, causing serious injuries. Once again the city council was on the verge of throwing out all Carnival and Mardi Gras celebrations by once again making them illegal.

As the adage goes, misfortune can and often does lead to good fortune. In relation to Carnival and Mardi Gras, this proved to be

Throwing brickbats and lime in place of sweetmeats.

the case. Instead of cancellation, the city's first organized Carnival parade group was about to be born. It was to become the foundation of our present-day celebration.

A group of cotton brokers from Mobile, Alabama, were working in New Orleans in 1856. They met at the Gem Saloon in the 100 block of Royal Street to discuss plans to organize a celebration for Mardi Gras that would serve to defuse the situation that existed. The young men, while in college in Mobile, had organized a New Year's Eve parade with floats, flambeaux and masked riders that proved to be highly successful. At the meeting, it was suggested that since the Mardi Gras parade was for revelers why not call the group "Comus" after the Greek God of Revelry. Another member liked the idea but suggested the name be given an American twist. To do this they agreed to spell Comus with a "C" and to spell crew "krewe" to give it a Greek flavor. Two floats were borrowed from Mobile along with flambeaux and costumes. Even though information about the first organized parade was publicized, not many people gave it much thought. The anticipated large crowd was not to be seen when the 8:00 p.m. starting time arrived. This was all to change, and to change very quickly. At precisely 8:00 p.m. on Mardi Gras February 24, 1857, on the corner of Julia and

Feb. 24, 1857
First Comus Mardi Gras Parade

Magazine Streets, two floats appeared. The first carried Comus the God of Revelry and the second a flaming volcano with Beelzebub in its mouth. The two floats were lighted by hundreds of "devils" carrying flambeaux. The skeptics, who had remained at home, upon seeing the sky light up as the parade progressed, thinking a massive fire had broken out and was spreading, were drawn to the area like moths to a flame. Someone was quoted as saying, "It was as though they came from within the bowels of the earth, for one minute they were not there and the next they were." The theme of the parade was "The Demon Actors In Milton's Paradise Lost". Paradise might have been lost, but new life for Mardi Gras began with the birth of the Krewe of Comus.

When the parade ended, the masked riders went to the Gaiety Theater. They were joined by 3,000 guests from New Orleans and Mobile. The jovial crowd witnessed New Orleans' first Mardi Gras ball that included tableaux for the entertainment of the guests. The parade and ball were even more successful than the men who planned it thought it would be. The newspapers wrote fantastic descriptions of both the colorful crowd-pleasing parade and fancy ball. If they had used a star rating at the time, it no doubt would have received five stars. Even Mark Twain, who was not the easiest man in the world to please, after attending the festivities, also wrote a great review of the first Mardi Gras parade in North America with floats, flambeaux and masked riders. Proof that you can't please everyone came when one French newspaper denounced Comus as being "composed of swine eating Saxons whose intrusion would bring an end to the city's Mardi Gras celebration." He simply had his nose out of joint. The first parade, although planned in the French Quarter, was not held there but in the American sector.

Today, because of the huge numbers of people who go into the French Quarter during Carnival and Mardi Gras, parades are allowed on the outskirts only. It is feared that if a parade were going down one of the main streets and a fire started, the necessary fire equipment would not be able to get in to fight the fire.

In recent years, Bourbon, Royal and a few other streets in the French Quarter are so crowded on Mardi Gras, if you were to pass out you would never hit the ground; you would simply be carried along with the shoulder-to-shoulder crowd.

FLOATS AND PARADES

MARDI GRAS FLOAT
CUTS THROUGH CROWD
LIKE SHIP CUTS THROUGH WATER

Ship cuts through the sea as Mardi Gras float cuts through a sea of humanity.

Mardi Gras floats have traveled the streets of New Orleans for 134 years. Early Mardi Gras floats were small, with just a few masked riders. More recent floats are much larger. Some could even be called "humongous".

The sizes, designs, and modes of propulsion for Mardi Gras floats have changed over the years. One aspect that has not changed since throws became an integral part of Mardi Gras parades has been the similarity of Mardi Gras floats of the streets of New Orleans and ships of the oceans.

Just as a ship cuts through the water lifting waves until it passes, Mardi Gras floats cut through the sea of humanity lifting a wave of arms until it passes.

NEW ORLEANS' LARGEST PARADE FLOAT

With New Orleans being the Mardi Gras Capital of the World, you would surmise that a Mardi Gras parade would contain the largest float.

WRONG!

City's largest float.

On April 12, 1860, a parade was held in honor of the unveiling of the statue of popular Henry Clay. The statue was located on the neutral ground on Canal Street between Royal and St. Charles Streets. The parade had only one float, but it was a whopper and a half. A 50-ton, three-mast sailing ship was taken out of the waters of the Mississippi River, placed on an undercarriage and pulled by a team of horses down Canal Street, around the statue and back to the river. As the ship moved down Canal Street, sailors raised and lowered the sails to the rhythm of the nautical music of the band that led the parade.

MARDI GRAS PARADE FEUD

In 1885, the Krewe of Comus, God of Revelry, cancelled its parade for a five-year period. In doing so, they relinquished their parade rights on Mardi Gras night. The reason was to give financial support to the Pickwick Club in furnishing their new quarters on Canal Street. Even though parades were not part of Comus's Mardi Gras celebration for the five-year period, the Pickwickians continued to stage beautiful and well-attended Mardi Gras balls for members and their guests.

In 1882, the Krewe of Proteus, God of the Sea, began parading during Carnival on the Monday night prior to Mardi Gras. When Comus discontinued their parade schedule, Proteus jumped at the opportunity to move to the more prestigious date on Mardi Gras night. All went well until 1890, when Comus decided to resume their parade schedule. Proteus was not about to relinquish their rightful place and declined to withdraw to make room for Comus. For the first time, both krewes were scheduled to ride on the same night. Because they were competing on the same night to the same audience, both krewes spent additional finances to gain the admiration of the spectators. With this fierce head-to-head competition, it was inevitable that they were to have a confrontation that night. On the night of the dual parade, Proteus reached Canal Street first. After rolling along the downtown side of Canal Street, they moved to the uptown side and headed toward Bourbon Street, where they were to turn and go to the French Opera House. When they reached Bourbon Street, the Krewe of Comus floats were blocking the intersection. All hell was about to break loose when the horse-mounted Proteus Captain made an attempt to cross over and cut the Comus procession in half. It would have been like Moses parting the Red Sea had the maneuver been successful. Instead, the hot-tempered Irish Captain of Comus, also mounted on horseback, galloped full speed until he got alongside the Captain of Proteus. He reached out and pulled the reins of the Proteus Captain's horse. The two men stared at

Comus and Proteus feud defused.

each other. The silence of the moment was deafening. Each
one's facial expression was of defiance. Next, heated words
broke the silence followed by impolite gestures. The Proteus
Captain declared he would lead his parade through the Comus
procession cutting it in half. The reply yelled back by the
Comus Captain was, "Over my dead body." Both men were at
the boiling point and ready to dismount and make their points
in a pugilistic manner. Before they could dismount, the masked
brother of the Captain of Comus, who was also a member of
Proteus, anticipating such trouble, grabbed the bridle of the
Proteus Captain's horse and led it away until the Comus parade
cleared the intersection. Once Comus passed, the Proteus procession proceeded to the French Opera House located on the
corner of Bourbon and Toulouse Streets. When the Comus
parade ended, the members attended their ball at the Grand
Opera House on Canal Street.

The street confrontation was only round one for the evening. The next obstacle that needed to be hurdled was in Rex's

hands. Who would he call on first? Rex trustees decided that Proteus should be called on first. Rex (Sylvester P. Walmsley) had a different idea. He surmised that since he was king, he would make the decision. He chose to call on Comus first. Rex and his beautiful queen, Nita Shakespeare, were greeted by the grateful God of Revelry and his followers with a fanfare of trumpets. As they were led to the throne, the orchestra played the traditional "Triumphal March" from Verdi's "Aida". Everyone was happy, at the Comus ball, that is.

Next on the agenda was Rex's visit to the Proteus ball at the French Opera House. The contrast there was like night and day. Word had gotten to the already angered Krewe of Proteus that Rex called on Comus before coming to them as he had done in previous years. The warm welcome and happy feeling enjoyed by everyone at the Comus ball was 180 degrees from the chilly reception Rex received at the Proteus ball. Proteus put off seeing Rex for such a lengthy time, Rex finally departed without the two meeting. Aside from a glass of champagne, chilled no doubt by the atmosphere, all Rex received that evening was a cold shoulder.

The evening of February 18, 1890, was long remembered for different reasons by Comus Queen Katherine Buckner and Proteus Queen Emma Jaubert. Of course, the names of the men who were Gods of Revelry and the Sea are not known because of krewe secrecy.

The friction generated on that fateful evening did not end that night. In making plans for the 1891 parade, Proteus members found out, through a rumor, that Comus would offer more than double the usual rental price of the prestigious French Opera House to secure it for their ball. Proteus counteracted by bidding $3,650. They were already beaten twice and would not be humiliated again. The information they received was erroneous. Many believed that rumor was started by Comus members. Proteus was not only the highest bidder; they were the only bidder. The Comus officers, no doubt laughing under their breaths or Mardi Gras masks, had already rented the Grand Opera House for a mere $1,000.

It has been 102 years since the Proteus/Comus street confrontation, ball procrastination and Comus's outfoxing Proteus in ball rental, yet you can bet your sweet bippy that when Mardi Gras enthusiasts get together, they still talk about that evening as though it was yesterday.

1953
REX AND COMUS SHARE THRONE

Rex and Comus share throne.

Only once in the city's colorful history have Rex and Comus shared a throne in a Mardi Gras parade. Wait a minute! The date of the parade was October 17th, and everyone knows that Mardi Gras can fall only between February 3rd and March 9th. To add to the confusion, the parade was held to celebrate the sesquicentennial of the transfer of Louisiana from France to the United States. Why then, you might ask, was it held on October 17th, not on December 20th, the anniversary day of the transfer. The reason for these bizarre circumstances is as follows: The sesquicentennial committee wanted President Dwight Eisenhower to be their honored guest. They were emphatic and would not settle for anyone else. After much correspondence, the committee persuaded him to attend. He advised he would be happy to participate, but the only open date on his busy calendar was October 17th.

On the chosen day, President Eisenhower watched from the reviewing stands set up directly across from Jackson Square as Rex waved his scepter and Comus his wine cup, both sharing one throne. Undoubtedly, President Eisenhower must have thought to himself, "Boy—this is really weird."

Of course, to make it all come out even in the end, yet another parade was held on December 20, 1953, this one without the President.

BIGGER FLOATS—BIGGER PROBLEMS

For many years, Carnival and Mardi Gras parades went through the heart of the French Quarter to the delight of the happy crowds. The narrow streets brought the crowds so close to the parade, it made the spectacle look larger than life. The dancing lights and shadows generated on the old buildings by the flambeaux made for a special atmosphere unobtainable on wide avenues and streets. Those fortunate to be on balconies were eye to eye with the masked riders as the floats passed. Some were so close that trinkets were literally and effortlessly exchanged from hand to hand.

The bottleneck for floats in the French Quarter was the close, sharp turn behind the Cathedral at the corner of Royal and Orleans Streets. At the intersection, the church had installed six steel posts set in concrete to discourage parking on the sidewalk. When floats were made bigger, it was soon realized that either the parades would have to move or the posts would have to be removed. The church officials were contacted and agreed to allowing installation of new posts that could be

unscrewed and removed on days of parades. The work proved
to be rather simple and the problem was solved. As the krewes
grew in numbers, so did the size of the floats. One of the innovations introduced to carry more maskers per float was the
building of the double-decker floats. That was the easier of the
solutions to accommodate more members. The other was a
doozie. The float length had to be extended to the extreme, so
much so that it could no longer make an easy turn at the intersection of Royal and Orleans. An ingenious system was
designed, using giant hydraulic jacks to help negotiate the turn.
The floats were literally picked up hydraulically and shoved

Hydraulic jacks help make sharp turn.

around the sharp curve. City officials decided finally that the
risk, in the event of a fire, was too great. Carnival and Mardi
Gras permits for parades passing though the center of the
French Quarter were discontinued. Had this decision not been
made, the parades using the longer floats would have had to
move anyhow. There was no way, including use of hydraulic

jacks, they could have made the sharp turn at Royal and Orleans.

Today, the longest floats built for a Carnival parade are well over 100 feet in length, not counting the tractor; that is over four times the length of the original floats. One float today can carry in excess of 100 masked riders. That is almost as many maskers as rode in an entire parade when all the parade madness began 135 years ago.

UNUSUAL PROBLEM SOLVED

Those masked riders who rode in the early years attested to the fact that one could get an intoxicating feeling during the parade after only one or two drinks. The phenomenon was caused by the riders recycling their own breaths inside a full-face mask. To alleviate the problem, a "breathing mask" was designed and implemented that has air slits cut in all the facial wrinkles allowing fresh air to be drawn in when breathing.

MOMUS
GOD OF LAUGHTER

Momus, one of the old line Mardi Gras krewes, was founded in 1872, the same year as Rex. In the first five years of their existence, they paraded on New Year's Eve, not during Carnival or Mardi Gras.

Momus, God of Laughter, gave everyone a good laugh in 1877 when they held their first Carnival parade. The float builder made a faux pas in building the floats wider than the doors of the den (a building where floats are constructed and stored). In order to get them out, they had to knock a wall down. The parade did not start until 10:00 p.m.

Float wider than den doors.

TOKEN MARDI GRAS PARADE

In 1942 and 1943, all traditional Carnival and Mardi Gras parades were cancelled because of World War II. Rex did have one float, with a serviceman as king.

As noted in the picture, the float was pulled by mules. You will also note that the people, out of habit, raised their arms as the king's float passed, even though nothing was being thrown.

World War II float with military personnel.

BREAKING TRADITION

In 1899, Proteus, God of the Sea, was forced to cancel its parade because of inclement weather. You would think that the God of the watery Sea would not allow water to cancel its parade, but it did. Realizing they were going to have to reschedule their parade, they had an emergency meeting and decided to parade the Friday after Mardi Gras (during Lent).

The parade did roll, but, to the krewe's amazement, the streets were virtually empty. Like the old lady in the hamburger commercial who said, "Where's the beef?", Proteus members said, "Where's the crowd?"

Yes, New Orleanians are truly traditionally minded people.

CAMARADERIE

Misfortunes through the years have struck individual parade krewes. Such an event was a fire in one krewe's den. All floats of the krewe were destroyed just two weeks before they were scheduled to parade. In spite of this mishap, the parade rolled as planned. Floats from other krewes were lent to the one who suffered the catastrophe so the people of New Orleans as well as the krewe members themselves would not be disappointed.

MARDI GRAS BALLS
INSTANT ROMANCE AT MARDI GRAS BALL

Mardi Gras has been known to generate a festive and happy feeling to the vast majority of its followers. In one instance, it cast a romantic spell on two of its faithful participants who saw each other for the first time while attending a Mardi Gras ball. Because of that chance meeting, a ghost dinner was served for many years on Shrove Tuesday night at a little known, but quaint, Royal Street restaurant. Strange as it may sound, the most popular dish for which the restaurant was noted was served every Mardi Gras for many years at a table with only memories, not people.

The romantic story happened many years ago when Mardi Gras balls were held in the French Opera House on Bourbon Street. One night, at the Comus ball, a young man from an eastern city paid absolutely no attention to the colorful tableau taking place on the stage. Instead, he was mesmerized by the beauty of a young Creole girl on the opposite side of the auditorium. Once he saw her he couldn't take his eyes off of her. After a long time, apparently sensing his staring, she looked his way. It seemed that when their eyes met she was powerless to look away. The young man smiled and the flicker of a smile was returned. He then rose and made some flimsy excuse to the friend that he was with and quietly strolled out into the empty lobby. With blind faith, he was positive she would join him. In a few moments, she walked into the lobby and quietly faced him without saying a word. Smiling down at her he suggested they leave together at once. She, as if in a trance, followed. While slowly walking hand in hand, she looked up at him and said, "By coming with you, you have ruined my reputation." He, without hesitation, answered, "If I have done that I will have to marry you, won't I? However, it might be a good idea if we first had dinner." The couple continued walking hand in hand down Royal Street. They went into the first restaurant they came to. The young man told the waiter that love had made him very hungry and that he should serve them the finest dish and wine the restaurant had to offer. The waiter responded, filling the order as requested. As they ate, the young couple told each other their names, about their pasts, and their wishes for their future lives. They spent the entire evening eating and drinking and just enjoying each other's company. The next morning, they went to the St. Louis Cathedral, attended mass, had ashes and then were quietly married by one of the parish priests. From there, they went to the young woman's home. A few days later, the couple went to live in his hometown in a northern state. Neither of them ever saw Mardi Gras again. Before summer arrived, the beautiful young bride of only a few months died.

The next Mardi Gras a startling development took place. A few days prior to Mardi Gras, the proprietor of the restaurant received money and a strange request through the mail. The letter requested that the same table be decorated with flowers and that the same foods and wines be served that were served the previous Mardi Gras. Each year that the young man lived, a letter with money was sent to the proprietor. When the young man passed on, money was sent to the proprietor through his at-

torney. He was advised that the young man had died, but the ghost dinners would go on until either the money he left in his will ran out or the restaurant closed.

Through the years the name of the restaurant and the names of the young couple have been lost. What has not been lost is the story of the unending love of the young couple who fell in love at first sight at a Mardi Gras ball many years ago.

MARDI GRAS BALL
FUTURE PRESIDENT OF THE UNITED STATES

Another story of love involving a Mardi Gras ball in the French Quarter is as follows:

A young professional soldier named Eisenhower stationed at Jackson Barracks attended a Mardi Gras ball and met a young lady and fell in love. Shortly after the chance meeting, he married her. The son that was born to the young couple was named Dwight, who we have all come to know as General Dwight D. Eisenhower and later President Dwight D. Eisenhower. Dwight is also the President of the United States who added the name of God to the Pledge of Allegiance. "One nation, under God, indivisible, with liberty and justice for all." For that we say, "Thank you and amen."

DON WE NOW OUR GAY APPAREL

Mardi Gras has been called the Harvard/Yale game of homosexuals. It is also the one opportunity in the whole year to legally go out in clothing of the opposite sex. The New Orleans Mardi Gras has a nationwide magnetic attraction for the gay crowd. It lures homosexuals from throughout the continent of North America as well as other parts of the world. There are motels that have 100 percent occupancy by these gay visitors. They pay for next year's room rental before leaving the current celebration.

There may not be as many homosexual Carnival balls as there are straight balls, but there is no comparison when it comes to the magnificence of the homosexual extravaganzas compared to the others. There is fierce competition between the various gay groups to see who can outshine the others. At one time, these balls were non-public, and to hide the identities of the participants they were held in out-of-the-way places. Today they are held in French Quarter hotel ballrooms, as well as auditoriums in New Orleans and surrounding parishes. At one time, the groups were limited to gay men. Through the years, things have changed. Some groups recruited gay women, and yet others claim that it also has some straight members. The gay krewes, unlike the straight organizations of Carnival, whose king and queen serve for one day, gay queens serve for an entire year. He (she) is accorded special honors at all the club functions. These functions are parties that raise the necessary funds for the next costly, extravagant ball. One club boasts of being so rich it does not have to stoop to that level to put on a first-class ball. They claim all of their parties, like their lavish balls, are simply for the enjoyment of its members.

Competition among the members of the gay krewes is furious. There is as much political jockeying for top positions as there is in the city's political arena. Members who participate in the balls will spend whatever it takes, be it time or money, to gain power or stand out in a crowd. One member who had to do a very short tap dance during a ball skit took tap dancing lessons for three months to ensure a memorable performance.

Gay balls have borrowed what has proven to be successful from the straight balls. They have themes, elaborate tableaux, call outs and beautiful invitations. One year, one of the clubs had the theme "Nicholas and Alexandra". The invitation sent out was an elaborate cardboard Faberge easter egg. Members that year entered the ballroom walking in their high heels and fancy gowns on a deep, soft, white carpet. This was done to show that the club had class.

Another ball was held in the Chalmette Auditorium with every seat taken. The theme was "Great Disasters of the Western World". The program started off with the auditorium and stage in total darkness. One could not see his hand six inches from his face. After a minute or two of total darkness and silence, eerie funeral and death music started very slowly and built to a uncomfortable level. The discomfort lasted for just a short time, just enough to get one's total attention, and then the level was reduced to where it could barely be heard. At that time, a spotlight was aimed at a coffin in the center of the stage.

Coffin with flower and candelabra.

On top of the coffin was a huge, magnificent, multi-colored floral arrangement. On each side of the arrangement stood a tall, three-pronged candelabrum. As the flower arrangement lifted, the level of the music was raised. The floral arrangement was the headpiece of the queen of the ball. When she stood erect, she walked to the side of the coffin. As she did, the two candelabra rose. They were the headpieces of the queen's attendants. As the music continued, each of the attendants walked to the center of the coffin, stopped and pulled the handles of the coffin, opening it into the queen's throne. The huge auditorium, packed to capacity, applauded in appreciation. For the next two hours there was nonstop entertainment with 19 different tableaux. Each depicted a great disaster. The number

Queen, two attendants and throne made from coffin.

of deaths inflicted by the catastrophe was given with each act. The numbers varied from a single death to 25 million. The single death was entitled "The King is Dead". Need we say more? This was depicted by a medley of hit songs sung and danced by an Elvis Presley look alike. Between the Rock and Roll King and the 25 million deaths claimed by the black plague that lasted from 1348 to 1666, were some unbelievable scenes. A few of the scenes depicted in three-dimension, multicolored, and acted out on the stage with appropriate background music, were the sinking of the Titanic, the Great Chicago Fire with realist fire and smoke effects, the fiery crash of the Hindenberg.

The homosexual ball is to many of the gay community the ultimate event of Carnival and Mardi Gras. It is every bit as exciting, if not more so, than the French Quarter Bourbon Street costume contest held annually. Many of the costumes worn by the members in the balls are also entered in the Bourbon Street competition. And, yes, they are always among the winners.

Mardi Gras is a time when everyone does his own thing. For many, many years, a Texas homosexual motorcycle club of approximately 100 members came to New Orleans to put on their own show in the French Quarter on Mardi Gras. One year, their theme was centered around Egypt. The pharaoh and his queen were carried through the streets on a gold litter in the skimpy yet elegant costumes in which each was clad. The pharaoh and his queen were carried by four jet black slaves who wore tiger skin mini briefs. Every so often, the parade would stop and the litter bearers would ceremoniously lower the pair to the ground.

When this happened, attendants, both men and women, also in tight, micro mini, skimpy costumes, poured wine from stone jars into the king's and queen's mouths. When they finished drinking, they were fed grapes and fancy food from a huge tray, as others played strange looking instruments of the period.

Homosexuality has been a part of Carnival since the time of Rome's world domination before the time of Christ. It is believed that costuming for Carnival was started by homosexuals of the Roman senate. As the members of the gay community might say today during carnival, "Don we now our gay apparel, for this is our day of days."

MISCELLANEOUS

ONCE A YEAR

In order to keep people (especially the inebriated ones), from climbing the steel poles that support galleries (porches) to get a better view of the festivities, it has always been common practice for businesses and residents alike to grease the poles as a means of keeping unwanted persons off of their balconies.

Poles greased to discourage climbers.

It has never been reported that anyone successfully reached the gallery by climbing a pole that was greased. In the earlier years, axle grease was used. Today vaseline serves as the deterrent. It is every bit as effective as axle grease and much easier to remove when no longer needed.

WEATHER

Just as the date of Mardi Gras can fall anywhere between February 3 and March 9, a period of 35 days, weather during Mardi Gras has also fluctuated. In recorded history, it has varied almost three times as many degrees as number of days.

The coldest Mardi Gras on record was on February 14, 1899 when the temperature dipped to a freezing 6.8 degrees. It also

happened to be the coldest day ever recorded in New Orleans history. The temperature has climbed to the low 90's on a number of occasions. This variation is close to a 90 degree swing. If nothing else, it proves that Mardi Gras is a swinging time, even in reference to the highs and lows of the weather.

Since Rex began parading in 1872, rain has cancelled their parade only once — 1933. Because New Orleans' weather records over the past 100 years show rain falls 32 percent of the days in February and 29 percent of the days in March, it is expected that some rain, even if not enough to dampen the spirits of the revelers, falls in the city on Mardi Gras approximately

one third of the time. To prove that it takes a lot to dampen the spirits of the revelers, the date of Mardi Gras in 1927 was on March 1. On that memorable day 2.12 inches of rain fell. In 1939, Mardi Gras was on February 21, when 1.69 inches of rain fell. In spite of the weather, Mardi Gras parades rolled as usual on both of these dates. Or, should I say, floated down the parade route.

The date of Mardi Gras 1895, was February 26. On February 14 of that year, New Orleans recorded its heaviest snowfall, 8.2 inches in 24 hours. In shaded places, the snow lasted a full week. Less than two weeks later, Mardi Gras parades rolled as usual.

No matter what the weather conditions are, be it wet or dry, sleet or snow, one thing is for sure — Mardi Gras is never a dry day when it comes to consumption of liquid refreshments.

SPECIAL ACCOMMODATIONS TO SATISFY DEMAND

WAREHOUSE AND GREAT ICE CHEST

It has been reported that some motels and hotels have used their swimming pools to ice down the beer necessary to satisfy the phenomenal demand during Carnival and on Mardi Gras.

The ever-popular Pat O'Brien's does a booming business during Carnival selling the world-famous Hurricane (a pinkish rum drink). They sell so many during the Carnival season it is necessary to rent extra warehouse space just to hold the empty glasses. Most of the visitors, when ordering a drink, buy the glass as well. After the drink has been consumed the glass is kept and taken home as a memento of their visit to Pat O'Brien's and Mardi Gras.

REX MARDI GRAS BEADS

In recent years, no doubt every New Orleanian and visitor who attended a Rex Parade has caught at least one pair of the highly popular special-made purple, green and gold beads. They are easily distinguished from other beads as they have a Rex medallion directly in the center. Take a moment and dig a pair out of your Mardi Gras memorabilia storage area. Every local family and those who have visited during Mardi Gras seem to have at least one. Chances are you will have little trouble finding a pair, since 792,000 pairs were thrown just in the year of 1988.

As you look them over, remember this mind-boggling statistic. Mr. Roger Wong, representative of the beads manufacturer in China, advised that the staff he assembled to fill the 792,000-pair order was made up of 600 people working in two 12-hour shifts, seven days a week, for two solid months. The reason it took so many to make them, each bead on every strand of the 792,000 is strung by hand, and the clasp on each end is tied by hand with a double knot.

BABY BOOM OF MARDI GRAS

During Carnival, more babies are delivered in Metropolitan New Orleans than in any other city in the world during the same number of days. A conservative estimate would be 500,000 plus.

What difference does it make if they are plastic babies delivered in king cakes? They are almost as welcome by New Orleanians as real babies. One grandmother compared them to grandchildren. You get all the fun and none of the responsibility.

HEAD OF MARDI GRAS!!!

Mardi Gras is in a sense a headless giant

This is truly one of the phenomenona of Mardi Gras. As big as the celebration is, there is no one leader, general manager or president. The city is responsible for crowd control and sanitation. The rest is coordinated by hundreds of different krewes who work independently of each other. It all works like clockwork because of the years and years of experience. The enjoyment received far overshadows the work and expense.

MUSIC

Music has been an integral part of Mardi Gras celebrations long before the first Comus parade in 1857. Yet, during Carnival and Mardi Gras, the New Orleans Philharmonic Orchestra leaves town to go on tour. Past attendance records prove it is unwise to compete with this ever popular celebration.

LAW

Because of Legislative Act 1924, Number 3, masking is allowed on Mardi Gras only from sunrise to sunset. The law prohibiting masking at any time other than Mardi Gras is as follows:

> "No person shall use or wear in any public place of any character whatsoever or in any open place in view thereof a hood or mask or anything in the nature of either or any facial disguise of any kind or discrimination calculated to conceal or hide the identity of their person or to prevent his being readily recognized."

POLITICS

It is quite unusual in New Orleans, where political figures have such great powers, that since 1872, when Rex was organized, there has only been one New Orleans mayor, Joseph Shakespeare, who was Rex in (1882). Because Mardi Gras clubs are private, with powerfully influential members, politics has never been able to get its tentacles into the inner workings of the old line Mardi Gras clubs of New Orleans.

The first real political attack against these groups was forthcoming in 1992. It was in the form of an ordinance passed by the City Council. The ordinance requires all private clubs to open their memberships to persons of any race, religion or gender by 1993. With the ordinance came the first shot fired allowing politics to get its tentacles into Carnival and Mardi Gras. Rest assured Mardi Gras faithful will not take it lying down. Let's hope the political shot does not bring Mardi Gras down.

HIGH HEELED TENNIS SHOES

Long before Nike had tennis shoes with a pump, Mardi Gras revelers wore real high heel pump tennis shoes.

High heeled tennis shoes.

BABIES REGISTERED AT BIRTH

The older Carnival club members take no chances of having their offspring left out of the Carnival festivities. To be sure that this does not happen, it is a well-practiced ritual that when a birth certificate has been acquired the child is immediately registered with the Carnival krewe with which his family is associated. This way they will hopefully someday have an opportunity of becoming part of the royal family of the krewe.

THE OTHER END OF THE SPECTRUM

Even though New Orleans is a democratic city in a democratic state in a democratic country, there are more kings and queens buried in New Orleans than any other city in the world. What difference does it make if they were only Mardi Gras kings and queens? To New Orleanians, this is serious business.

TUXEDO CAPITAL OF THE UNITED STATES

It is true that New Orleanians are called easygoing folk. And, yes, they are known to enjoy life. It is also true that they work as hard as they play. When they work, they dress accordingly and when they play they dress to the hilt.

New Orleanians, per capita, because of the city's cultural and Carnival seasons, own more tuxedos than any other city in the country.

New Orleans 4.1 per thousand
New York 3.1 per thousand
San Francisco 2.9 per thousand
Chicago 2.4 per thousand

Even though tuxedos are sold today in a variety of styles and colors, the old standby — black — is still the number one choice.

Tuxedo capital of the U.S.

MARDI GRAS DATES FOR THREE CENTURIES
1801 - 2100

The following is a list of the dates, and number of times Mardi Gras was or will be held on each date:

February			February		
	3 -	1	21 -	10	
	4 -	2	22 -	11	
	5 -	3	23 -	10	
	6 -	6	24 -	12	
	7 -	8	25 -	7	
	8 -	6	26 -	11	
	9 -	8	27 -	13	
	10 -	10	28 -	10	
	11 -	11	29 -	2	
	12 -	12	March 1 -	12	
	13 -	8	2 -	10	
	14 -	9	3 -	10	
	15 -	10	4 -	10	
	16 -	12	5 -	9	
	17 -	11	6 -	8	
	18 -	11	7 -	4	
	19 -	8	8 -	3	
	20 -	9	9 -	3	

February 3rd is the earliest and March 9th is the latest date Mardi Gras can occur.

From 1801 to the present, Mardi Gras has been celebrated on March 9th twice, in 1886 and 1943. Both of those years Comus, the city's oldest krewe, did not parade. Mardi Gras will once again fall on March 9th in 2038. Is it possible that with the pending ordinance reference private clubs, Comus will not parade in 2038, or any other year for that matter?

MARDI GRAS DATES FOR THREE CENTURIES

1801 Feb. 17	1838 Feb. 27	1875 Feb. 9	1912 Feb. 20
1802 Mar. 2	1839 Feb. 12	1876 Feb. 29	1913 Feb. 4
1803 Feb. 22	1840 Mar. 3	1877 Feb. 13	1914 Feb. 24
1804 Feb. 14	1841 Feb. 23	1878 Mar. 5	1915 Feb. 16
1805 Feb. 26	1842 Feb. 8	1879 Feb. 25	1916 Mar. 7
1806 Feb. 18	1843 Feb. 28	1880 Feb. 10	1917 Feb. 20
1807 Feb. 10	1844 Feb. 20	1881 Mar. 1	1918 Feb. 12
1808 Mar. 1	1845 Feb. 4	1882 Feb. 21	1919 Mar. 4
1809 Feb. 14	1846 Feb. 24	1883 Feb. 6	1920 Feb. 17
1810 Mar. 6	1847 Feb. 16	1884 Feb. 26	1921 Feb. 8
1811 Feb. 26	1848 Mar. 1	1885 Feb. 17	1922 Feb. 28
1812 Feb. 11	1849 Feb. 20	1886 Mar. 9	1923 Feb. 13
1813 Mar. 2	1850 Feb. 12	1887 Feb. 22	1924 Mar. 4
1814 Feb. 22	1851 Mar. 4	1888 Feb. 14	1925 Feb. 24
1815 Feb. 7	1852 Feb. 24	1889 Mar. 5	1926 Feb. 16
1816 Feb. 27	1853 Feb. 8	1890 Feb. 18	1927 Mar. 1
1817 Feb. 18	1854 Feb. 28	1891 Feb. 10	1928 Feb. 21
1818 Feb. 3	1855 Feb. 20	1892 Mar. 1	1929 Feb. 12
1819 Feb. 23	1856 Feb. 5	1893 Feb. 14	1930 Mar. 4
1820 Feb. 15	1857 Feb. 24	1894 Feb. 6	1931 Feb. 17
1821 Mar. 6	1858 Feb. 16	1895 Feb. 26	1932 Feb. 9
1822 Feb. 19	1859 Mar. 8	1896 Feb. 18	1933 Feb. 28
1823 Feb. 11	1860 Feb. 21	1897 Mar. 2	1934 Feb. 13
1824 Mar. 2	1861 Feb. 12	1898 Feb. 22	1935 Mar. 5
1825 Feb. 15	1862 Mar. 4	1899 Feb. 14	1936 Feb. 25
1826 Feb. 7	1863 Feb. 17	1900 Feb. 27	1937 Feb. 9
1827 Feb. 27	1864 Feb. 9	1901 Feb. 19	1938 Mar. 1
1828 Feb. 19	1865 Feb. 28	1902 Feb. 11	1939 Feb. 21
1829 Mar. 3	1866 Feb. 18	1903 Feb. 24	1940 Feb. 6
1830 Feb. 23	1867 Mar. 5	1904 Feb. 16	1941 Feb. 25
1831 Feb. 15	1868 Feb. 25	1905 Mar. 7	1942 Feb. 17
1832 Mar. 6	1869 Feb. 9	1906 Feb. 27	1943 Mar. 9
1833 Feb. 19	1870 Mar. 1	1907 Feb. 12	1944 Feb. 22
1834 Feb. 11	1871 Feb. 21	1908 Mar. 3	1945 Feb. 13
1835 Mar. 3	1872 Feb. 13	1909 Feb. 23	1946 Mar. 5
1836 Feb. 16	1873 Feb. 25	1910 Feb. 8	1947 Feb. 18
1837 Feb. 7	1874 Feb. 17	1911 Feb. 28	1948 Feb. 10

1949 Mar. 1	1987 Mar. 3	2025 Mar. 4	2063 Feb. 27
1950 Feb. 21	1988 Feb. 16	2026 Feb. 17	2064 Feb. 19
1951 Feb. 6	1989 Feb. 7	2027 Feb. 9	2065 Feb. 10
1952 Feb. 26	1990 Feb. 27	2028 Feb. 29	2066 Feb. 23
1953 Feb. 17	1991 Feb. 12	2029 Feb. 13	2067 Feb. 15
1954 Mar. 2	1992 Mar. 3	2030 Mar. 5	2068 Mar. 6
1955 Feb. 22	1993 Feb. 23	2031 Feb. 25	2069 Feb. 27
1956 Feb. 14	1994 Feb. 15	2032 Feb. 10	2070 Feb. 11
1957 Mar. 5	1995 Feb. 28	2033 Mar. 1	2071 Mar. 3
1958 Feb. 18	1996 Feb. 20	2034 Feb. 21	2072 Feb. 23
1959 Feb. 10	1997 Feb. 11	2035 Feb. 6	2073 Feb. 7
1960 Mar. 1	1998 Feb. 24	2036 Feb. 26	2074 Feb. 27
1961 Feb. 14	1999 Feb. 16	2037 Feb. 17	2075 Feb. 19
1962 Mar. 6	2000 Mar. 7	2038 Mar. 9	2076 Mar. 3
1963 Feb. 26	2001 Feb. 27	2039 Feb. 22	2077 Feb. 23
1964 Feb. 11	2002 Feb. 12	2040 Feb. 14	2078 Feb. 15
1965 Mar. 2	2003 Mar. 4	2041 Mar. 5	2079 Mar. 7
1966 Feb. 22	2004 Feb. 24	2042 Feb. 18	2080 Feb. 20
1967 Feb. 7	2005 Feb. 8	2043 Feb. 10	2081 Feb. 11
1968 Feb. 27	2006 Feb. 28	2044 Mar. 1	2082 Mar. 3
1969 Feb. 18	2007 Feb. 20	2045 Feb. 21	2083 Feb. 16
1970 Feb. 10	2008 Feb. 5	2046 Feb. 6	2084 Feb. 8
1971 Feb. 23	2009 Feb. 24	2047 Feb. 26	2085 Feb. 27
1972 Feb. 15	2010 Feb. 16	2048 Feb. 18	2086 Feb. 12
1973 Mar. 6	2011 Mar. 8	2049 Mar. 2	2087 Mar. 4
1974 Feb. 26	2012 Feb. 21	2050 Feb. 22	2088 Feb. 24
1975 Feb. 11	2013 Feb. 12	2051 Feb. 14	2089 Feb. 15
1976 Mar. 2	2014 Mar. 4	2052 Mar. 5	2090 Feb. 28
1977 Feb. 22	2015 Feb. 17	2053 Feb. 18	2091 Feb. 20
1978 Feb. 7	2016 Feb. 9	2054 Feb. 10	2092 Feb. 12
1979 Feb. 27	2017 Feb. 26	2055 Mar. 2	2093 Feb. 24
1980 Feb. 19	2018 Feb. 13	2056 Feb. 15	2094 Feb. 16
1981 Mar. 3	2019 Mar. 5	2057 Mar. 6	2095 Mar. 8
1982 Feb. 23	2020 Feb. 25	2058 Feb. 26	2096 Feb. 28
1983 Feb. 15	2021 Feb. 16	2059 Feb. 11	2097 Feb. 12
1984 Mar. 6	2022 Mar. 1	2060 Mar. 2	2098 Mar. 4
1985 Feb. 19	2023 Feb. 21	2061 Feb. 22	2099 Feb. 24
1986 Feb. 11	2024 Feb. 13	2062 Feb. 7	2100 Feb. 9

OFFICIAL AND UNOFFICIAL END OF MARDI GRAS

Just as there is an official beginning of the Carnival season on January 6th, there is also an official and an unofficial ending of Mardi Gras.

Official and unofficial end of Mardi Gras.

OFFICIAL

Just prior to midnight of Mardi Gras, Rex's officers and royalty join Comus and his queen at their ball. Rex and Comus escort each other's queen in a grand march. At the end of the march, which is at midnight, Rex waves his scepter, officially bringing Mardi Gras to an end for another year.

UNOFFICIAL

At approximately the same time, an unofficial ending of Mardi Gras takes place in the French Quarter. This one is on Bourbon Street. A wall-to-wall carpet of humanity is reminded by the men in blue, mounted on horseback, as they slowly walk down Bourbon Street in a wedge configuration. Following the mounted police are water trucks with powerful sprays of water washing the trash to one side, followed by street sweepers with powerful mechanically driven brushes sweeping up the trash. Behind them are empty trucks accompanied by men from parish prison picking up the tons and tons of trash and loading it into the empty vehicles. The efficiency and precision with which the French Quarter is cleared and cleaned is almost as interesting and colorful as any Carnival or Mardi Gras parade.

BIG BASH
GENERATES TRASH AND CASH

You have heard the old saying, "one man's trash is another man's treasure." In reference to Carnival and Mardi Gras in the Metropolitan New Orleans area, this is so true.

As one would expect, the bigger the crowd the more trash. It is also a truism that in hotter weather more trash is generated than in colder weather.

I thought it would be a good idea to put together a chart that would graphically show the amounts of trash and the corresponding economic impact for the same year. I still think it is a good idea, but I found it to be impossible. Each sanitation department in each parish has a different method or no method at all to give factual figures in reference to the amount of trash collected during the Carnival season. To further complicate the situation, garbage and trash are of course different things. Although we do read articles in the newspaper after every Mardi Gras as to the amount of trash collected, I have, after lots and lots of digging (not through the trash), been unable to come up with anyone who would say, "This is the official amount of trash collected during the past 10 years."

In trying to put together a chart on the economic impact per year, this was like opening a can of worms. Each and every office or person contacted had a different method of determining the economic impact and of course the figures varied by many, many millions of dollars.

Unless the city appoints one person or department to determine the economic impact on Carnival and Mardi Gras, we will no doubt remain in the dark. In reference to the trash generated, unless citizens are charged by the pound to have it picked up, this unknown will remain unknown.

CROWD ESTIMATIONS

This opens another can of worms. Of all the people contacted, I have yet to find anyone who is responsible for estimating crowds and the formula by which they determine the figure.

CHAPTER 6

DELIVERY TO YOUR DOOR

GOOD OLD DAYS

Delivery To Your Doorstep

Today we think we have it made with supermarkets and shopping centers. We have delivery to our doorstep of hot pizza pie, cold milk and even beauty products by the Avon lady.

In years gone by, much of what you needed was made available to you by street vendors. You could be anywhere in your house or even in your backyard, and you knew immediately what street vendor was in your neighborhood. Street vendors in the French Quarter are a tradition as old as the Vieux Carre itself.

Almost every conceivable product or service you needed, if you were patient, would, in time, be in front of your house. Some products you purchased, because of necessity, on a daily basis. Others you purchased less frequently. Some were only seasonal. The products and services brought to your doorstep were made available by vendors who used every means conceivable. Some walked, carrying baskets in both hands, plus huge, loaded baskets on their heads. Some used pushcarts, while others rode in wagons drawn by mules and finally gasoline-powered motor vehicles.

Just as there were various ways of bringing their products and services, there were a multitude of means of gaining your attention once they were in eyesight or earshot of your house. To attract your attention, the first and most frequently used was the vendor's verbal cry, called singing. Some of the colorful, attention-getting and ingenious cries are to be found later in this chapter. Besides their strong voices, they used tin horns, bugles, cymbals, bells, whistles, and even a metal triangle that was rung by striking it with a piece of steel.

There were three good reasons why street peddlers were popular. The first was convenience. Second, because of lower overhead, they were able to sell for less than store prices. And finally, the food products were often fresher than what you could get in stores.

Today we take for granted services that are the necessities of life; gas, water and electricity are just a few examples of what services we receive automatically today.

Since it is a known fact that men can live longer without food than he can without water, let us start there.

WATER MAN

AT FIRST, WATER WAS HAULED FROM THE RIVER AT 50¢ A HOGSHEAD~

Because water is one of the real necessities of life, one of the very first street vendors to be found in the French Quarter was the water man. Water, prior to purification plants, came directly from the Mississippi River; the water man not only delivered, but also prepared it for human consumption. The process by which this was done was as follows:

Wooden containers called hogsheads were filled with river water. Once filled, each container received a bucket of coal and a small scoop of alum. When these two items were placed in the container, the water was vigorously stirred with a paddle and then left to settle overnight. The next day, the water was delivered, and the user dipped water from the top. Once the water level got close to the bottom, where the sediment collected, it was time to start another container.

The next time you go to the faucet to get a glass of water, just think of the effort it took our forefathers to do that simple task.

COAL AND WOOD MAN

Coal and wood

Washing clothes today is not something you even give a second thought to. You just load the machine, put in some soap powder and push a few buttons. In the days prior to automatic washing machines and gas dryers, street vendors were there to help you. They delivered wood, and later coal, to stoke the furnace in the backyard where clothes were boiled.

Before the days of natural gas, wood and coal were also used to heat the homes and cook the food. Every home had enormous iron stoves with brick furnaces built directly into the chimney. Wealthy home owners had wood or coal fire grates in every room. Those less fortunate had one, two if lucky, to heat the entire house.

One of the favorite cries for this vendor went—
Char-coal! Charcoal!
My horse is white, my face is black.
I sell my charcoal, two bits a sack—
Char-coal! Charcoal!

KINDLING MAN

Kindling

Another important vendor was the kindling man. Kindling is small strips of thin wood that was used to help start a wood or coal fire. The vendor spent hours cutting the kindling and then bundling it. Once this was done he was ready to carry it to his potential customers. The kindling man would also offer his service to cut wood at the customer's home. The charges varied, but it was 50 cents a cord for many years. A cord equals a stack of lumber measuring four feet by four feet by 8 feet.

CLOTHES POLE MAN

When the clothes were washed, the next street vendor needed was the clothes pole man. The washed clothes were placed on lines that ran between two points—sometimes between trees or from the fence to the house, or other combinations. Once the clothes were secured to the line, they were lifted into the air with a pole so the wind could hit them and dry them quickly. Clothes poles were made from trees or branches of small diameter. They always had a fork on one end that fit the clothesline to support it.

CHIMNEY SWEEP

Chimney Sweep

Each of the fire grates to heat the home and the stove to cook the food required a chimney. If you let your chimney get clogged, you were in for serious trouble. A clogged chimney would not only fill your house with smoke, but could cause a fire.

In the early days of the French Quarter, chimney sweeps were in high demand, and they knew their business. Chimney sweeps were easy to spot. They were a colorful lot wearing tall, battered silk hats and swallowtail coats. They carried the tools of their trade with them at all times and had a colorful cry to gain attention.

Ra-mi-eau! Ra-mi-eau! Ra-mi-eau!
Lady, I know why your chimney won't draw,
Oven won't bake and you can't make no cake,
An' I know why your chimney won't draw!
Sweep'em clean! Sweep'em clean!
Save the firemen lots of work,
We hate soot, we never shirk,
Sweep'em clean! Sweep'em clean!

Chimney sweeps would continue to sing as they worked. The reason—to let anyone who might be below him know that the chimney was being cleaned and to stay clear of the fireplace so as not to be showered with soot.

KNIFE AND TIN MAN

Knife and scissors man

If you were anywhere in your home and you heard a four-note whistle, you knew the knife and tin man was in your neighborhood. The whistle was a shrieking, high-pitched instrument that got your attention even if the dogs were barking, which they usually did when they heard the irritating sound. If you were in front of the house, you could also see him from a far distance. He carried on his shoulder a grindstone mounted on a wheelbarrow-like frame that reached high into the air. On his head was a tin hat, which was symbolic of the work he could perform; namely, repairing tin products (before the days of synthetic products) that many of the housewives used everyday in preparing meals. On his chest was a tool box, chock-full of the needed tools to grind scissors and sharpen knives. He could also sharpen handsaws, make keys, and do other miscellaneous repair work that might be needed.

This vendor took no chances on being missed by potential customers. As he worked he rang a small bell that was attached to the leg of the grindstone frame.

RED BRICK DUST VENDOR

Not all houses in the French Quarter had front steps (also called stoops). Those that did, purchased red brick dust from elderly women or small boys who dominated this trade. Stoop sitting was a daily event prior to air conditioning and television. It was the place where all family members congregated to entertain themselves.

Vendors would pound soft red bricks into fine, dark red powder. They then sold this to housewives who used the powder as a bleach. Each Saturday, it was a ritual in the French Quarter to clean the front steps by using the red brick powder. The clean front step was a proud symbol of good housekeeping. No housewife worth her salt left this chore undone. Unlike the inside of the home that not many people saw, the stoop was right out front where everybody could and did inspect the condition of the step.

UMBRELLA MAN

Umbrella Man

New Orleans, with close to 60 inches of rain annually and showers almost every day in the summer, umbrellas are a necessity in every household.

Most people who purchased an umbrella used it for as long as repairs could be made. This was one service vendor who did not do the repair work on the site. The reason—it was impossible to carry all the tools necessary to repair all umbrellas. When as many umbrellas were collected that could be carried on his back, the vendor headed to his shop, made the necessary repairs and returned them to the customers. He then began collecting more broken umbrellas where he had left off.

ICE MAN

Last Home Ice Delivery Service 1946

New Orleans being semitropical, prior to mechanical refrigerators the ice man was at your door, every day during the summer and less frequently during the winter months. He did not have a whistle, a horn, or a cymbal; he just checked the area of the house where the ice was to be delivered. There was a preset system whereby the customers let him know how many pounds were needed. He would deliver the product in most instances without ever seeing his client.

In the summer months, this vendor was one of the most popular delivery men for children. He drew them to his wagon like a magnet. The attraction—each time he cut a piece of ice with his ice pick from the large 300 pound block, children, like vultures, swooped onto the back of the wagon and picked up the slivers of cold, refreshing, free ice.

BOTTLES, BONES AND RAGS

Bottle, bones and rags

The bottles, bones and rags man was a unique vendor by the fact that he did not charge you. Instead, he paid you for collecting items he would purchase and then resell. Children collected bottles that held beer, whiskey, champagne, condiments, relish, etc. All bottles, with the exception of medicine bottles, because it was illegal to reuse them, were on his list for purchase. The bottle man blew a horn to gain attention. When he gave off a loud blast in the neighborhood, it was like the Pied Piper of Hamelin. Children ran from every direction carrying sacks, boxes, bushel baskets and anything else they could find to carry the products the vendor wished to buy. Once they were face to face, the bargaining began. The vendor would pay money, but reluctantly. He would barter with the children long before he would shell out cash. To entice them, the lower section of his wagon always had a drawer filled with trinkets that every child wanted and could not live without. It was said that his collection, although all small items, was more varied than those delivered by Santa Claus at Christmas. The vendor would pull the bottom drawer open and it would be filled with tops, rattles, horns, whistles, beads, toy soldiers, as well as many different kinds of candies. The children's aim was to barter for as many items as possible for their booty. The bottle man's position was to give as little as possible. Some were naturally better at bargaining than others. Those who were not as good watched and gained expertise in bargaining for the next time the bottle man came.

Children seemed to dominate bottle collecting while adults who received money for their items controlled the rags and bones end of this venture.

Note: Bones were used in the manufacturing of soap.

FOOD VENDORS

Because New Orleanians have always lived to eat and not merely eat to live, food vendors were by far the most popular to work the streets of the Quarter.

You would have to think long and hard to find a food item that was not made available at one time or another. Today, most visible of the existing street vendors is the Lucky Dog man. Although they do not go house to house as was the custom of vendors of old, they can be found at numerous street intersections throughout the Quarter.

A food critic was quoted as saying reference the Lucky Dog (tongue in cheek), "This had to be the best meal in the Quarter; ten thousand flies couldn't be wrong."

CALA

Cala Lady

One of the early as well as popular food vendors in the French Quarter was the cala lady.

Cala:

Pastry—thin fritter made with rice and yeast sponge.

Since prepared yeast in the early years was not available, yeast was concocted by boiling potatoes, adding corn meal, flour and cooking soda. After this mixture was left overnight to ferment (usually outdoors), it was then mixed with boiled rice and made into a sponge. Once this was completed, flour, eggs, milk and butter were added and mixed thoroughly. The last step to complete the process was the forming of the calas by dropping spoonfuls in deep, hot fat.

Since the calas were mostly served as a breakfast food, cala women were heard in the streets early in the morning. They made their way carrying huge wooden bowls on their heads, chock-full of warm, fresh calas. If you got a whiff of the aroma, you could not resist the cala lady.

To be sure their presence was known, the following is one of the numerous cries the cala women used:

Calas, calas - all nice and hot
Calas, calas - all nice and hot
Lady, me I have calas!
Laaa-dy, me I have calas!
All nice an' h-o-t . . .
All nice an' h-o-t . . .
All nice an' h-o-t. . . .

For many years, the cala lady was a permanent fixture outside the Church of St. Louis. This was a great place to sell her wares. It was the custom for citizens to receive news of the week after church service in front of the church on the square.

Even though the cala women no longer walk the streets, calas are still sold in restaurants in the French Quarter.

To add even more flavor to the already flavorful cake, restaurants today sprinkle powdered sugar on top and offer cane syrup on the side. Talk about finger-licking good!

WAFFLE MAN

Waffle Man

When you heard a bugle bring forth sweet melodious sounds, you knew immediately it was the waffle man. His product was such a delicacy, upon hearing the waffle man's bugle, customers didn't walk, they ran to his wagon.

The waffle man's cry was as follows:

The waffle man is a fine old man.
He washes his face in a frying pan.
He makes his waffles with his hand,
Everyone loves the waffle man.

The waffle man was like the man who wears suspenders and a belt. He made doubly sure of accomplishing his goal. If for one reason or another you did not hear his cry, his bugle was sure to get your attention.

PIE MAN

Besides waffles, some vendors walked the streets with hot pies of various flavors. Some of the favorites were lemon, apple, chocolate and banana. When strawberries, blackberries, blueberries and other local fruits were in season they were sold in place of the standard flavors. As we all know, variety is the spice of life. The pie vendors sure knew how to spice up the taste buds of their customers and have them come back for more.

MILK MAN

Milk Cart

The milk man is another of those vendors as old as the city itself. Milk was a perfect marriage for pastries, so the milk man stayed close behind the cala and the pie vendors whenever possible.

The first milk vendors roamed the streets in two-wheeled carts carrying two huge galvanized milk cans. One held milk, the other buttermilk. The two large, bright, brass-bound cans were carried in the front of the wagon, necessitating the drivers standing much of the time in order to see the road. In the early days, when a customer came to the wagon and placed an order, milk was dispensed from spigots at the bottom of the can into the buyer's container. Besides milk, the great New Orleans delicacy (according to my taste buds) Creole cream cheese was also peddled from these carts.

At a later date, milk was delivered in glass bottles. Prior to milk being processed in plants where it was homogenized, the cream would always be found at the top in the neck of the bottle. Before being poured, the bottle had to be shaken vigorously to mix the fat with the milk. Children used to get up early in the morning, take the paper stopper off of the bottle, stick their fingers into the neck and get a taste of the rich cream.

Since the milkman made early deliveries, many families were awakened by the clanging of the bottles as he made deliveries. To some it was irritating; to most it was a welcome sound.

SNO (SNOW) BALLS

Snoball Man

It is true that you will not find what New Orleanians call snoballs listed in the dictionary. It is also true that snoball vendors covered the streets of the French Quarter in the hot, humid months like sunshine covered the streets. Although it is not known how or who came up with the term "snoball", supply catalogs listed equipment to make snoballs in the 1800s. Snoballs are as much New Orleans as red beans and rice, gumbo, or the poorboy sandwich.

While snoballs have no nutritional value, and are sprinkled with sugarcoated calories by the thousands, they have been sought after in the Quarter by the masses, because they are colorful, tasty, good, and on hot, humid summer days, especially before air conditioning, they were the number one means of cooling off.

Snoballs have to be in a category all by themselves when it comes to popularity. Snoball vendors did not have a specific cry, ring a bell or toot a horn. They relied on the best advertising means known to man—word of mouth. Once a vendor sold a few customers, the satisfied customers did the rest.

It is interesting to note that the three most popular colors/flavors are purple/grape, green/spearmint and gold/lemon. These are the three colors of Mardi Gras. A coincidence—perhaps.

FRUIT AND VEGETABLE VENDOR

The greatest variety of products, of all the street vendors, were sold by the fruit and vegetable peddlers. Their carts groaned under the weight of their colorful and eye-pleasing cargoes. Carrots, onions, artichokes, okra, and mustard greens were some of the vegetables. Bananas, oranges, grapes, watermelons, cantaloupes and apples were just a smattering of the fruits sold. Fruits, along with the vegetables, were displayed on the wagons and carts just as supermarkets display them today. Vendors knew that displaying played a large part in generating sales. It made the products pleasing to the eye and sometimes irresistible.

Watermelon plugged upon request.

Not only was the fruit displayed in a colorful manner, samples were also made available in order to consummate a sale. To help generate the sale of serpent-striped melons, along with various shades of green, watermelons were cut in half and displayed to show how red, sweet and juicy they were. If a customer requested that a melon be plugged, that meant the vendor would stick a long knife in the very center of the melon, cut out a triangular plug, stick the knife into the plug, take it out and let the customer have a taste. Many a watermelon were sold in this way. Cantaloupes were not plugged for sampling, but one, or more if needed, was cut into slices for the customer to taste before buying.

Street Criers

Most of the street vendors, when crying out their songs, used the following procedure:

They would cup one hand and place it over one ear. In the other ear they would place a quarter. They would then cup their other hand, placing it against the side of their mouth that had the quarter in the ear, and sing their song. The quarter and the hand in front of their mouth served in a sense as ear plugs.

The following are a few examples of watermelon, cantaloupe and mixed vegetable cries:

WATERMELON

I got water with the melon,
Red to the rind!
If you don't believe it
Jest pull down your blind.
You eat the watermelon
and pree-serve the rind!

CANTALOUPE

Cantal-ope-ah!
Fresh and fine,
Just offa de vine,
Only a dime!

VEGETABLES

Nice little snap beans,
Pretty little corn,
Butter beans, carrots,
Apples for the ladies!
Jui-ceee lemons!

LOCAL SPECIALTY FRUITS

When the fruits were in season, older men and women, along with young children, spent hours upon hours picking

Blackberry Man

blackberries, strawberries, dewberries, Japanese plums, persimmons and figs. The peddlers then took to the street working in pairs. One would be on each side of the street. Once they started on their route, one would sing his cry, and, when finished, the partner would then sing. After this was done, they would sing in unison. The procedure was repeated until someone stopped them to make a purchase.

> Blackber-reees! Fresh an' fine.
> I got blackber-reees, lady!
> Fresh from th' vine!
> I got blackberries, lady!
> Three glass fo' a dime.
> I got blackberries!

OYSTER MAN

New Orleanians have always had a love affair with the mighty oyster. As one man said, when looking at the unappetizing, somewhat repulsive raw oysters, "It had to be one hungry dude who ate the first one, and am I glad he did."

The oyster man was no slouch when it came to calling attention to his product. Because his product didn't last long without refrigeration, he had to work doubly hard to sell them as quickly as possible. One of his cries went:

Oyster man! Oyster man!
Get your fresh oysters from the Oyster Man!
Bring out your pitcher, bring out your can,
Get your nice fresh oysters from the Oyster Man!

FISH MAN

Fish Vendor

Because of necessity, fish vendors were the pushiest of all food vendors. Prior to ice being available, products not sold the day it was made available to the customers for the most part had to be discarded. The fish salesmen were good, but every potential customer had a nose that told them if the fish was fresh.

After spending the necessary time to make the catch, these vendors did everything within their power, even if it required being obnoxious, to sell the fish.

Even after ice was available to help preserve the unsold fish, these peddlers retained their hard sell tactics. Habits, both good and bad, are hard to break.

A good example of the hard sell tactic used by the fish peddlers is shown in the following article run on April 4, 1889, in the Daily Picayune.

> "During the Lenten season, when fish are in great demand, the basket peddlers of the finny product do an excellent business, especially in selling the inferior kinds of fish. The wares are not always of the freshest and many cases are on the very verge of decomposition, yet they succeed in imposing upon the careful housewife or servant by stout protestations that their fish are perfectly fresh . . . They ring at doorbells and if not promptly answered jerk the wires as though they will pull the bell from its fastenings. A simple refusal to purchase incenses them, and they thrust the offensive smelling fish in the faces of persons, and if they still refuse, frequently give vent to curses and abuse of those whom they seek to impose on."

PLANTATION SLAVES AS STREET PEDDLERS

"I Got Creole Corn, I Got Creole Tomatoes"

A great number of plantation owners were known to be frugal. Some people even went so far as to label them downright cheap. As one man put it, "Some plantation owners are so tight they squeak when they walk." One example of their frugality is as follows: In order to continue receiving a return on their investment in slaves too old to work in the fields, the older slaves were often sent to town to peddle surplus crops. It had to be profitable, for the plantation owners did not complain when they were required to purchase licenses for their slaves to do this chore.

It is possible, I feel highly probable, that this practice of sending plantation slaves to sell surplus products house to house was where the great confusion of the meaning of the word "Creole" came into play. Today in mixed company, when you mention the word Creole, it is like opening a can of worms.

The confusion of the word Creole came about as follows: The plantation owners told their slaves that the products they were to sell door to door were to be hawked as Creole products, as they come from the Creole's plantation. This indicated, like the Creole's themselves, the products were the crème de la crème. The slaves did their jobs well, selling Creole corn, and Creole tomatoes. Almost every vegetable and fruit was labeled Creole. It went so well that when a plantation owner sold one of his mules they were even touted as Creole mules. The slaves, seeing how well this was received and being owned by a Creole plantation master, they called themselves Creole slaves.

The original meaning of the term Creole, as defined by the Spanish who introduced the term to New Orleans is as follows:

CREOLE

A white descendant of the French and Spanish settlers in Louisiana. The word came from the Spanish word criollo, believed by the proud Spanish people to mean, "From the thigh of Jupiter!" Crème de la crème, pure blooded. No break in the blood line.

As noted in the above information, the word Creole started out as a noun and little by little was converted into an adjective. The fact is there is so much confusion as to what a Creole is today; Webster's dictionary has a multitude of meanings for the word. As it stands today, almost anything, or anyone can fall into the category of a Creole.

Chances are that many of the old Creoles are not only turning in their graves, but spinning like tops.

FIRST IN U.S.

HOME DELIVERY FROM RETAIL STORE

Daniel H. Holmes began his highly successful retail store operation in 1842 on Chartres Street. He later moved the operation to a larger building on Canal Street on the edge of the French Quarter.

Holmes was a successful department store proprietor many years before A.T. Stewart began operating in New York advertising his store as the first department store in America.

Daniel Holmes was a man ahead of his time. He was the first to hire females to be retail clerks and the first to sell ready-to-wear ladies' clothes. One of his popular innovations that spread from coast to coast began in 1845, three years after he went into business. During the Mexican War, many Army officers and their families were stationed in New Orleans. The officers' wives felt as if they were in heaven whenever they shopped in Holmes's department store. The only problem was that the road to the barracks was dark and lonely. The ladies, in carrying their purchases back to the barracks, feared robbers. Mr. Holmes, upon learning of this, began a new service to his customers—free home delivery. This service proved to be so popular it was copied by stores throughout the country.

DELIVERY — IN 1845! DEPARTMENT STORE

SUNDAY
OPEN FOR BUSINESS NOT NEW

Open for business on Sunday not new.

The following is taken from John Williamson Crary, Senior's memoirs entitled "Reminiscences of the Old South From 1834 to 1866", chapter "The Crescent City".

"My first impressions of its peculiarities seemed to me like a sudden transfer to some strange foreign city. It was on Saturday about the last week in January, 1835, that we arrived at the flatboat landing of New Orleans. Next morning after late breakfast, I concluded to walk out and see my first quiet Lord's day of rest in a Louisiana city. As soon as I got out in a street I saw the drays, wagons and carts going and coming in every direction. As I proceeded I saw the stores open and the people in their business garbs and habits seemed to be using the most extraordinary energy and anxiety. I said to my companion, 'We have lost a day, this must be Monday.'

" 'No,' he replied, 'this is the day for everything and everybody in New Orleans.'

"As I proceeded through the French Quarter on Levee Street, the gambling and liquor saloons were all open and in full blast. The steamboats were discharging and receiving cargoes, the drays were hauling cotton, sugar and upper country produce, the markets were all open and full of people, the military companies were parading the streets. The whole scene was unique, grotesque and profane. It was neither a gala day nor a carnival, but a heterogeneous composition of all that human tongue, action and motive could inspire for selfish and material gratification. The desecration of the Sabbath was never a crime in New Orleans and, until the Northern and Southern people of the old states took the lead, which was about 1850, Monday looked more like the Lord's day than Sunday."

As the old saying goes, "History does have a way of repeating itself."

Even though this chapter has come to an end, it is in no way a complete listing of all of the products and services that were brought directly to homes in the French Quarter.

To list just one more home service that is sorely missed today, and hopefully will one day be reinstated, is the family doctor. Doctors of the old days not only made house calls, but knew all members of the family and could call all of them by their first names.

That is what you call "the good old days".

CHAPTER 7

JACKSON SQUARE

INTRODUCTION

GOOD NEWS, BAD NEWS

19TH CENTURY BIG ON TEMPORARY STRUCTURES
1825 ARCH DE TRIUMPH
1826 50TH ANNIVERSARY SIGNING OF DECLARATION
OF INDEPENDENCE
1832 JOY AND SORROW
1847 ZACHARY TAYLOR

NINE O'CLOCK CANNON

IDEAS THAT NEVER CAME TO FRUITION

SQUARE'S TWO GREAT CONTROVERSIES

FOUNTAINS

STATUES

SECRET VAULT IN BASE JACKSON MONUMENT

LIKE GOOD WINE—BETTER WITH TIME

PLACE d'ARMES/JACKSON SQUARE

INTRODUCTION

In May of 1718, Governor Bienville arrived and marked off the spot where the capitol of Louisiana would someday be located. He named the city in honor of Monseigneur Duc d' Orleans, who was then Regent of France. The six ships in Bienville's expedition carried carpenters and laborers (former convicts), who were sent to clear the land and construct the city's first buildings. Bienville did not stay, but returned to Mobile.

On March 29, 1721, Bienville along with Adrien de Pauger, returned to New Orleans to carry out chief engineer Pierre La Blond de la Tour's plan for the city. When they arrived very little, aside from clearing the land and building a few unpretentious buildings, had been accomplished.

The earliest known map of the city, drawn by Le Blond de la Tour, is dated April 22, 1722. The map projected a simple grid of streets with a public square (present day Jackson Square) in the center. To show the importance of the area the land flanking the square was marked with a fleur-de-lis, indicating the land was reserved for royal use. The land facing the square was marked off to be the site of the parish church. De Pauger went about laying out the streets for the new city. It was four square blocks extending in each direction above and below the public square and six blocks parallel to the river.

Those who built structures prior to de Pauger's arrival, not knowing of de la Tour's master plan, built wherever they pleased. When these structures were found to be in the way, de Pauger order them moved. Most owners complied, but a few protested. In a document dated September 5, 1722, de Pauger related how he handled the sticky situation. His simple solution was to use a big branch from a tree and beat those who complained over the head when they protested. Is that how the Le Branch family got its name? Naw!

That same year, while visiting New Orleans, Father Charlevoix, a French Canadian priest, wrote the following:

"The town is the first that one of the world's greatest river has seen risen on its banks . . . but there are only huts placed without much order. A large warehouse built of wood and two or three warehouses that would not grace a French village . . . this wilderness that canes and trees still cover almost entirely, will one day, and perhaps that is not far off, be an opulent city in the metropolis in a great and rich colony."

The good father's prediction was right on the money. To get the ball rolling, once the streets and public square had been laid out, the next step was the parcelling out of land to the settlers to build their homes and businesses. The one condition was they enclose the property with palisades (earth works) and open along the street a ditch to serve as a drain for river water in times of inundation.

From the very beginning the square was the heart and pulse of the community. It had been classified, because of the varied uses and numerous historic events that transpired there, to be the most historic square of ground not only in New Orleans, but in Louisiana as well. Over the years it has been called by various names and its uses have changed even more frequently. On the

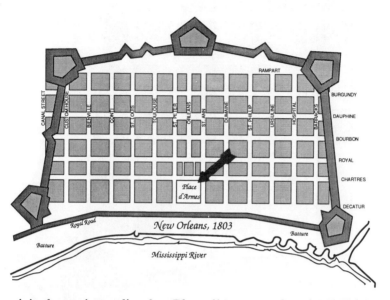

New Orleans, 1803

Mississippi River

original map it was listed as Place d'Armes. After the Spanish occupied New Orleans its name was changed to Plaza de Armas. Many of the old Creoles called it Place Publeque. The Americans, upon arriving after the Louisiana Purchase, called it the Public Square. It wasn't until 1851 that it was given its present name, Jackson Square, in honor of Andrew Jackson who distinguished himself in the brilliant victory he won at the Battle of New Orleans. There was considerable disagreement amongst the city leaders when the name was changed to Jackson Square. There was firm opposition. A highly vocal group wanted it listed as Jackson Gardens.

Note:

This was not the first site to be called Jackson Square. Prior to the Battle of New Orleans, Jackson reviewed his troops as they passed Fort St. Charles, present site of the old U.S. Mint on the corner of Esplanade and Chartres. When the fort was torn down, the area became a park. One of the many honors bestowed on Jackson after the victory was the naming of the square Jackson Square.

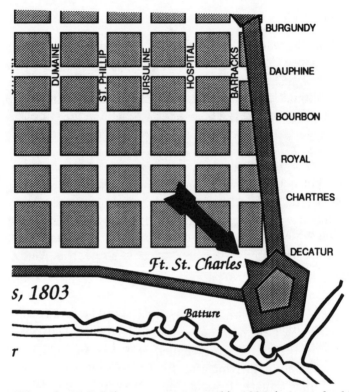

When the U.S. Mint was constructed in 1835, it was a double blessing, for the park had long since grown over with weeds and had become a dumping ground for one and all.

Through the years Jackson Square, like the heart of a human, has pumped volumes and volumes of not blood but historical data into the city's history books. Many of the happenings are what de la Tour had in mind when he selected the location and named the square Public Parade Ground. Chances are he did not fathom some of the cynical events that were to transpire over the 272 years of the square's existence.

This chapter will contain a variety of events, be they good bad or indifferent. This chapter could also easily be listed as "Sometimes Unusual, Sometimes Unbelievable, Sometimes Unique, But Always Entertaining."

GOOD NEWS - BAD NEWS

Like the fellow who said, "I have good news and I have bad news, which do you want first?" Usually the reply is, "Let's save the best news for last."

Although the square was to be a public parade ground where people could meet, mingle and pass the time in pleasant surroundings, it didn't take long for the square to be used for other less pleasant purposes.

In 1729, at Fort Rosalie, an outpost of the city, Natchez Indians killed 250 French settlers. The sneak attack would not go unanswered. The intention of the French government was to exterminate the tribe. In March of the following year, a female of the Natchez tribe was captured and transported to New Orleans. Historian Charles Gayarre wrote the following reference the incident:

> "Governor Perier allowed them to burn her in a great ceremony on a platform in front of the city between the city and levee (Place d'Armes). I regret to relate the whole populace of New Orleans turned out to witness that Indian ceremony. The victim supported with the most stoical fortitude all the tortures that were inflicted upon her and did not shed a tear—on the contrary—she upbraided her torturer with their want of skill. In flinging them every opprobrious epithet she could think of. She prophesied their speedy destruction."

It was later reported that the burning of the female Indian was the first in North America. Indian tribes who captured females of opposing tribes either killed them or sold them as slaves. The burning may have been the first, but it was not to be the last. Later that year Governor Etienne de Perier reported to the French hierarchy that he had captured 50 more Natchez Indians. He reported that he burned four men and two women at

Female Indian burned at stake.

the stake. The balance of those captured were sent to St. Dominque.

These were not the only executions to take place in the square. Many of the penalties of those punished for crimes were carried out in the square. For minor infractions the offenders were taken to the square and locked into a stock. They were required to sit facing the Cabildo from sun up to sunset. So everyone would know what crime they were guilty of, a large poster hung around their necks listing their name, offense, and the number of days of the sentence. It also listed who the culprit

Stock used for criminals.

offended. The punishment proved to be very effective. With few exceptions, most who were sentenced left town once they were freed.

Major offenders, to put it lightly, were treated very harshly. In fact, if you feel that today's punishment is minimal for the crimes committed, the following is probably one of the reasons the pendulum has swung so far in the opposite direction for those found guilty. In January 1766, Michel Degout was convicted of murder in Natchitoches. He was brought to New Orleans for a review before the superior council. They rendered the following decision:

> "premeditated murder, committed with a sculptor's chisel, on one Cratte, in reparation of which has condemned and condemns him to make honorable amends, barefooted and gowned, a rope around his neck, holding in his hands a flaming wax torch weighing two pounds, to be led to the main entrance of the parochial church of this city, where he will be

brought by the public executioner in a tumbril [cart], with a poster bearing on it 'Murder and Assassin' in front and back, and there bareheaded and on his knees to declare that he wickedly, with premeditation, murdered said Cratte, for which crime he is repentant and begs forgiveness of God, of the King and of justice; after which, in the same cart he is to be led by the public executioner to the public square [Place d'Armes] of this city, to have his arms, legs, thighs and back broken on a scaffold which, for this purpose, shall be erected on the said square, and he shall afterwards be placed on a wheel, to expire there with his face turned to Heaven until death ensues, his body be to then borne to and exposed on the public road . . .''

This type of punishment was not only local, but was carried out in all countries of the (western) world. Degout in one respect was lucky. Even though the sentence as described was carried out, records indicate he was strangled to death before the mutilating blows and exposure to the elements were carried out.

Another ghastly sentence was to have the guilty party nailed alive in a coffin and then cut the coffin in half. These were just some of the grotesque forms of punishment that took place in the square.

There was one more spectacular incident that took place in the square that led to an unpleasant finale worth noting before we proceed to more pleasant happenings.

When Louisiana was made a gift from the French government to Spain in 1762, the locals were not in any sense of the imagination jumping with joy. To the contrary, they felt betrayed and acted like a hen whose chicks were being molested.

Although the transfer officially took place in 1762, it was not until 1766 that Spain sent Don Antonio de Ulloa to serve as its first governor. Because it took four years to accept the gift—it makes one wonder if they really wanted it. We do know the Frenchmen living in the French Quarter and other parts of Louisiana did not receive Ulloa with open arms.

Even though the proud locals had four years to calm their frustrations and tempers, it proved not to be enough time to heal the hurt they felt. A secret group of conspirators made up of business, military and political leaders met in secrecy. Their unanimous decision was to rid themselves of the spineless Spanish governor. Through a concerted effort they determined to proudly return Louisiana to France, their confidence bolstered by the fact that Ulloa had only 90 soldiers under his command. This small force was too weak to command much respect. When all the logistics were worked out, a convention was scheduled in New Orleans. Prominent and powerful men from all over the territory answered the call. Joseph Villere made his grand entrance into the square leading 400 heavily armed German soldiers. When all who had been summoned had arrived, they assembled around the flagpole in the public square. After they finished discussing their options, the unanimous decision, once again, was expulsion of Ulloa and all Spaniards from Louisiana. The Superior Council asked Ulloa to leave Louisiana. Fearing bloodshed, he and his wife were taken aboard a vessel by his cohorts in the harbor. Historical facts are not clear as to whether he sailed on his own or if the ship was set adrift by inebriated men who had been at a wedding.

The entire incident, although full of emotion and great anxiety, was carried out without one drop of blood being spilled.

BLOODY O'REILLY

It is true that not one drop of blood was shed during the expulsion of Governor Ulloa, but the humiliation he endured was far worse and would not be left unanswered. Retaliation was swift and thorough. General Alessandro O'Reilly was selected to lead the armada to retake Louisiana. He was a tough, seasoned, unbeaten, professional, Irish soldier who was in the service of the Spanish government. Just as the brave Frenchmen were confident they could take back what was theirs, since Ulloa had only a handful of men, O'Reilly was equally sure he could retake what Spain rightfully and legally owned. His confidence of success was backed by 23 transport vessels carrying 2,600 men with firepower capability never before seen in this part of the world. O'Reilly's troops outnumbered the entire citizenry of New Orleans.

The best description of the arrival of O'Reilly was written by noted historian Charles Gayarre.

"At five o'clock in the afternoon, a gun fired by the flagship gave the signal for the landing of the Spaniards. The French troops and the militia of the colony, with [Acting Governor] Aubry at their head, were already drawn up in a line, parallel to the river and in front of the ships, in part of the public square [the Place d'Armes] which is nearest to the church of St. Louis. On the signal being heard, the Spanish troops were seen pouring out of the fleet in solid columns, and moving, with accurate precision, to the points which had been designated to them. These troops, numbering 2,600 men, were among the choicest of Spain, and had been hand-picked by O'Reilly himself.

"With colors flying and with the rapidity of motion of the most practiced veterans, they marched on, battalions after battalions, exciting the admiration and the awe of the population by their martial aspect and their brilliant equipments.

"The heavy artillery drew themselves up in perpendiculars, on the right and left wings of the French [troops], thus forming three sides of the square. Then came a heavy train of artillery of fifty guns, the light infantry and the companies of mounted riflemen (fusilieros de montanas), with the cavalry, which was composed of forty dragoons, and fifty mounted militiamen from Havana. All these corps occupied the fourth side of the square near the river, and in front of the French, who were drawn up near the cathedral.

"All the vessels were dressed in the colors, and their riggings were alive with Spanish sailors in their holiday apparel. On a sudden, they gave five long and loud shouts of Viva el Rey (Long Live the King), to which the troops on the square responded in a similar manner. All the bells of the town pealed merrily; a simultaneous discharge from the guns of the twenty-four Spanish vessels enveloped the river in smoke; with emulous rapidity, the fifty guns that were on the square roared out their salute, making the ground tremble as if convulsed with an earthquake; and all along the dark lines of the Spanish Infantry flashed a sheet of fire, as the weaker voice of musketry, also shouting in jubilation, attempted to vie with the thunder of the artillery. All this pomp and circumstance of war announced that General O'Reilly was landing.

"He [O'Reilly] soon appeared in the square where he was received with all the honors due a captain general; drums beating, banners waving, and [a band] playing, stirring sounds, causing the human heart to leap and the blood to run electrically through the hot veins.

"He was preceded by splendidly accoutred men, who bore heavy silver maces; and the whole of his retinue, which was of the most imposing character, was well calculated to strike the imagination of the people.

"With a slightly halting gait, he advanced toward the French governor, who with the members of the Council and all the men of note in the colony, stood near a mast which supported the flag of France . . .

" 'Sir,' said O'Reilly to Aubry,'I have already communicated to you the orders and credentials with which I am provided, to take possession of the colony, in the name of his most Catholic majesty, and, also, the instructions of his most Christian majesty, that it be delivered up to me. I beg you to read them aloud to the people.'

"Aubry complied with this request and then, addressing the colonists by whom he was surrounded said:'Gentlemen, you have just heard the sacred orders of their most Christian and Catholic Majesties, in relation to the province of Louisiana, which is irrevocably ceded to the crown of Spain. From this moment, you are the subjects of his Catholic Majesty, and by virtue of the orders of the King, my master, I absolve you from your oath of fidelity and obedience to his most Christian Majesty.'

"Then turning to O'Reilly, Aubry handed to him the keys of the gates of the town. The banner of France sunk from the head of the mast where it waved and was replaced by that of Spain."

Once this was accomplished, the next step was to put into action a vehicle necessary to punish those responsible for the misdeed. With one quick swoop, O'Reilly abolished the French Superior Council and substituted the Illustrious Cabildo. This new governmental body was partly a legislative and partly a quasi-administrative council similar to that in other provincial towns under Spanish rule.

Once the Cabildo was functional, an independent investigation was ordered to seek out the ringleaders. The report showed 12 men were the foundation and moving force behind the uprising.

They were all brought to trial with the exception of Joseph Villere, the same Frenchman who led 400 German troops into the city. While being held in prison on a Spanish ship, his wife came and tried to get his release. When he heard her voice, he bolted in an effort to get to her and was run through by a Spanish bayonet. He was tried in absentia, since he was dead.

The Frenchmen's defense rested on blaming Governor Ulloa, whom they claimed had not presented his credentials and taken official possession before exercising his rightful authority. General O'Reilly, every bit the gentleman, listened intently. When the trial was completed, six of the men were sentenced to death and six to imprisonment.

O'Reilly wished to bring the matter to a head as quickly as possible, but ran into a snare. There was not at the time an executioner in town to carry out the death sentence. A Negro executioner was available, but was disqualified from officiating upon whites. O'Reilly had overcome everything else and found a quick solution to this bottleneck. He modified the execution by hanging, to shooting. Although the penalty was modified, he had the infamy of hanging retained in the decree.

Note: Had the hanging been carried out, it would have taken place in the square for all to witness. The further humiliation of hanging was the sentence requiring that their bodies remain hanging until otherwise ordered.

The incident came to an end at 3:00 p.m. on August 25, 1769, when the execution by firing squad was carried out in the barracks yard. The description of the execution witnessed by the sheriff was as follows:

"At three o'clock the prisoners were taken from their places of confinement in the quarter of the Regiment of Lisbon and tied by the arms, were conducted by a good and sure guard of officers and grenadiers to the place of execution where a large body of troops stood formed in a hollow square. The sentence was then read to them in French and English. They were then put in position and fired upon."

This was the first attempt of one government to overthrow another in North America. It preceded the American's fight for freedom by scores of years.

The names of the men executed were:

Lafreniere - Mihet - Marquis - Noyan - Caresse

Villere - even though already dead was represented at the trial by an "abocat à sa memoire".

Although he was not executed, his sentence condemned him to perpetual infamy.

The six men who were imprisoned lost all of their worldly goods to the Spanish throne as did those who were executed, were as follows:

Petit—life

Douceten and Massan—12 years

Milhet, Poupet, and Hardy de Boisblanc—6 years

Note: Prior to the execution on August 25, all those who were condemned protested being tied to a stake to no avail. The Spanish were running the show. At the last moment O'Reilly displayed an act of compassion by offering the young, handsome and recently married Noyan his life if he would abandon his companions. He refused. He did make a request of O'Reilly that was granted. He asked that the scarf that was worn around his neck be given to his wife so that she might pass it on to his son when he became a man. He further requested that his son be told that to be a man, one must stand for what he believes in, even if it means death.

With nothing left to be done, the brave Frenchmen stood proud and erect. The Spanish rifles were lifted and aimed and

October 25, 1769, Lafreniere gives command to fire.

when all was ready, Lafreniere, the principal leader in the overthrow of the Spanish government gave the command to fire. The explosion of musketry announced the end of the revolution. August 25, 1769, was the darkest day the city had ever known.

As is proven over and over in history, misfortune for one is always good fortune for another. O'Reilly did his best to make amends for his part in the uprising. Even though he was tagged with the dubious title of "Bloody O'Reilly," he knew as a professional soldier he would not be endeared to those he offended in carrying out his military objective. To soften the blow, he donated to the city in the name of his royal master all the vacant lots on each side of the square (the site of present day Pontalba Apartments). He also showed leniency by punishing only 12 of those involved in the overthrow, even though hundreds could have been rightfully punished. O'Reilly went even further in beautifying the square that the Creoles so loved. The Spanish proved to be superb administrators and in time made conditions in the city much better than they had ever been under French rule. O'Reilly did many positive things for the people. Most of all he did little to disrupt their character, speech and customs.

19TH CENTURY

BIG ON TEMPORARY STRUCTURES

Even though there are permanent installations such as statues and monuments in the square, there have been equal numbers of temporary structures. These temporary items were for important celebrations. Prominent people who were honored in some of the more noteworthy celebrations included Andrew Jackson, Zachary Taylor, Marquis Lafayette, P.G.T. Beauregard, George Washington, Thomas Jefferson, and John Adams.

The temporary structures were huge and impressive. They included a replica of the Arc de Triomphe, an obelisk, facade of Buena Vista, and a doric column.

1825

ARC DE TRIOMPHE

With his first name being Marie, maybe that's why General Marie Joseph Paul Yves Roch Gilbert du Motier Marquis de Lafayette became such a great fighter and military leader. Fight he did on behalf of the Americans in their struggle for freedom from the English. The American government was so pleased with his military genius on their behalf, they offered him the position as first governor of Louisiana. Lafayette was a man who knew his capacity. He realized his strength was military and not political and graciously declined the offer. In 1825, many in the city—still being of French blood—were pleased when they learned Lafayette would be visiting New Orleans. Just as the general held no punches in aiding the American's cause, those who loved Lafayette in New Orleans would not hold their punches in honoring this great man. The first honor they bestowed on him was to empty out the Cabildo (at the time serving as City Hall) and turn it into his residence for the six days he would be in the city. The itinerary made for Lafayette would not only entertain him, but keep him busy every moment he was awake. Elaborate dinners, operas, parades, and teas were just some of the offerings. As someone stated, they would have to put starch in his underwear to help keep him going during his stay.

Possibly the greatest of his honors was enjoyed on the day of his arrival. Arriving by ship at the Chalmette battle site, he was greeted by Louisiana Governor Henry S. Johnson. From there a lengthy parade with many military groups and state dignitaries led by the general, made its way to Place d'Armes. When the head of the parade approached the square, the church bells began pealing. The huge crowds in the streets and on the roofs of the buildings waved their handkerchiefs as they shouted, "Viva Lafayette, viva Lafayette." The cheering reached a deafening pitch by the time they reached the square. Just as Lafayette reached the entrance to the square a battery of cannons fired in salute. When the general looked toward the square and saw what had been done for him, he was visibly moved. In the center of the square stood a 68 foot high, 58 foot wide, 25 foot deep replica of the Arc de Triomphe that had been erected in his honor. Although it was made of wood and canvas, it was painted to look like green marble. Only by close inspection could one tell if it was real or make believe.

Figures representing justice and liberty were painted on the base. Adorning the arch were two allegorical forms with trumpets and ribands depicting fame and bearing the names of Washington and Lafayette. At the very top was a statue representing wisdom above a bust of Benjamin Franklin. When Lafayette reached the arc, Mayor Phillippe de Roffignac, still a Frenchman to the bone, although an American citizen, was there to officially welcome the general to the city. It was reported that by this time the welcoming noise was so loud the mayor, realizing Lafayette could not hear him, simply pointed to an inscription, which stated in both English and French, "A grateful republic consecrates this monument to Lafayette."

At the time the hero of three revolutions was being honored

1825
Arc De Triomphe

in New Orleans, he was 68 years of age. Chances are, the short time he spent in the square under the Arc de Triomphe, being showered by praises from thousands of grateful Orleanians, was his greatest hour. It was the tallest structure ever built in the square.

1826
50TH ANNIVERSARY OF THE SIGNING
THE DECLARATION OF INDEPENDENCE

For the 50th anniversary of the signing of the Declaration of Independence the city decided to honor two great Americans and revolutionary heroes, Thomas Jefferson and John Adams. By coincidence both died on July 4, but years before the anniversary date of the signing of the all-important document. Just because their bodies had already been entombed months before the planned celebration made no difference. The council's enthusiasm was not dampened. They went ahead and made plans to hold a funeral without the corpses. The service was scheduled to take place in Place d'Armes August 14, 1826. For the great event the entrance to the square was draped in black. Erected in the center of the square was a huge stage. Projecting upward from the stage was a 25-foot square Doric column. On

Doric column.

the side of the column were painted the words "Union, Justice, Liberty and the Force". A replica of the Declaration of Independence was also displayed on two Cenotaphs (shape of horizontal grave stones). Attention was drawn to them by decoration of black plumes and wreathes made of oak and laurel. The final embellishment were busts of the two patriots.

The morning of the ceremony, at sunrise, the quiet of the morning was disrupted by cannon fire. This salute was continued every 30 minutes throughout the day. All vessels in port flew their colors at half mast. At 2:00 p.m. all businesses were required to close, at which time church bells throughout the city tolled. At 5:00 p.m. the funeral procession, including a horse-drawn funeral cart, without benefit of corpses, proceeded down Canal Street led by the United States Infantry, the Louisiana Legion and the Louisiana Guard. When they arrived at City Hall (Cabildo), the troops formed a double open line and presented arms as the funeral procession passed. When all who took part entered the square and those who were to be seated were accommodated, the solemn services began. The highly successful and lengthy event ended when a 24-gun salute served as a signal for the crowd to disperse, which they did with much reverence and dignity.

Even though the entire day was a huge success, not everyone was totally pleased. Bernard Mandeville Marigny, the irrepressible Creole was a little taken aback. He was almost certain the council would ask him to deliver the eulogy on Jefferson in his fluent and eloquent French. He was quite sad when he learned that Mayor Derbigny was given the distinction of carrying out that part of the program. His spirits were somewhat lifted when he learned the Louisiana State Gazette newspaper had agreed to print and run his undelivered remarks even though it was three days after the event.

1832
GEORGE WASHINGTON

The two major events held in the square in 1832 began with a happy celebration and ended in sorrow. The strange thing was that many participated in both events. All paid tribute in the first and many were recipients in the latter.

In the first, George Washington, the father of our country, was honored on February 22, 1832, the centennial of his birth. At daybreak the celebration began with a thunderous volley of cannon fire. As a special tribute, all ships in the harbor hoisted their flags in salute. Later that day a long, colorful, spirited, patriotic military parade took place. The galloping sounds of the horses' hoofs, the pounding of the feet of the soldiers along with the drum beat attracted all in hearing range to this special event. It was later noted in the local newspapers that the soldiers on parade should make the people who crowded the square proud. After reviewing them, the people could boast of a legion of troops equal to any in the world.

After the parade, special services were held in the Cathedral. To show the importance of the day, the choir sang the Te Deum, an ancient hymn of praise. Not one, but two lengthy human hymns of praise were also delivered, one in French and the other in English. Both told of the glories of the father of our country.

The sun finally set and the city lay in darkness, but the darkness didn't last long. In short order the entire square gleamed as though God had beamed down on this particular section of the city. Illumination appeared to be everywhere. Place d'Armes glimmered like a jewel that sparkled when the sun hit it. The fence rail all around the square was aglow by thousands of candles and bright torches. Thousands of additional candles were placed in the trees and on the elevated platform to accommodate the musicians in the center of the square. The light generated by the torches and candles was great enough that the musicians had no trouble reading their musical scores.

Candle and torch lit square, 1832.

There is something special about a lone candle flickering in the darkness. It has the capacity of mesmerizing its admirers. Multiply that feeling by thousands upon thousands and it will give you only a fraction of the enjoyment that must have been the pleasure of those who attended the centennial celebration of the father of our country.

HAPPY 50TH
TO SORROWFUL FIRST

Hundreds of those who attended the February 22nd celebration stood in the shadows of the candles and torch lights not knowing that many stood in the shadow of death. In 1832, the city's history was to be recorded as the tragic year. During the summer and fall many were to fall and never rise again lest it be to their place of eternal rest.

The citizenry at the end of summer and early fall were perplexed by the latest epidemic. It was a frightful experience that they had not before encountered. Cholera was the latest disease to show its deadly fangs. The people were panic stricken. True there had been other horrible diseases such as yellow fever, but the locals felt they had built an immunity and visitors normally bore the brunt of the deadly statistics. Cholera was a beast of another color. It paid no heed to locals versus visitors. It struck young, old, rich, poor, local or visitor, with equal intensity. The epidemic took a horrendous toll on all. In a 10 day period at the end of October and the beginning of November, 5,000 souls lost the battle for life to this new demon of death.

With so much misery being suffered by so many, the city fathers were at odds as to whether to schedule the annual Battle of New Orleans celebration. For many years the celebration was held on December 23rd because that was the anniversary date of the first combat of the Battle of New Orleans that culminated on January 8, 1815. The final decision was to hold the annual celebration and incorporate in it a funeral service for the victims of the epidemic. For the special occasion the talents of city surveyor, J. Pillie, were called upon. He designed an

elevated platform reached by five steps. From the steps rose an obelisk that soared 60 feet into the air. It was painted and decorated to give the appearance of white marble. As reported later in the newspaper it was most realistic looking, until you felt it and realized it was only canvas. On each of the four sides was inscribed in four languages:

SACRED
To The Memory Of Our Fellow Citizens
who died during the epidemic

To accommodate the religious services an altar was built in front of the monument.

At exactly 10:00 o'clock on the morning of December 23, 1832, the combination celebration of the Battle of New Orleans and memorial service for the dead began. The square was crowded to the point that if a person fainted there would not be a place on the ground to lay him down. Bishop Leo de Neckere performed religious service. The orator for the occasion was a city official. As was customary for the times, his speech was both flowery and lengthy. It was reported the next day in the newspaper that the speech was, "long enough to surely tax the feet of his standing audience."

1847
HERO'S WELCOME FOR ZACHARY TAYLOR

The only resident of Louisiana to be elected President of the United States was Zachary Taylor. His plantation was located on the east side of the Mississippi River north of Baton Rouge. When he resided there, the map listed the area as Spithead Point, Louisiana. He also had a home in Baton Rouge, located on the present-day state capitol grounds. Today the exact spot is pointed out by a marker. However, there is one small problem: the plaque is behind some shrubs in the capitol gardens and unless you know where to look, it is most difficult to find.

Old "Rough and Ready," as he was affectionately called, was the toast of the entire country in 1847. He was enjoying the limelight as conquering hero of the Mexican-American War. When he returned to Louisiana from his victory, it was unanimously decided he should be given a hero's welcome in the city of New Orleans. A committee was formed and planned what they labeled an unusual program to welcome their idol. The program began with — what else — a parade. In fact, there were to be not one, but two.

The first was to be nautical. The general and his entourage were picked up at nine o'clock on the morning of December 4th at Jackson Barracks. He was taken aboard the Merry Kingsland as the band played "Hail to the Chief". Once they were underway, steamer after steamer decked out in red, white and blue fell in line en route to the French Quarter. The line of steamboats carrying human cargos and no freight, included the America, Missouri, Convoy, Majestic, Caldonia, Sommerville, Panther, Colonial Clary, Gretna and St. Louis. When the ships reached Place d'Armes, Zachary Taylor was taken on deck from which he witnessed on shore a sea of humanity. Not only were the levees and streets packed to capacity, many had climbed to the tops of buildings with no regard for their safety. Their only interest was to get a glimpse of the hero that had honored their city with a visit. Lining the river were ships, four deep, from all parts of the world. The masts were crammed with sailors who climbed to all available spots to see old "Rough and Ready."

The Merry Kingsland passed the square and continued upriver as far as the city of Lafayette, now the Garden District. This was done so everyone would have a chance to see their idol. The ship then turned around and headed downriver. It docked opposite Place d'Armes.

Once the ship was secured the general was then led to the square, a monumental task since the crowd around the square was estimated to be 40,000. A cannon salute greeted Taylor, who was then escorted by military guard into the square where a Triumphant Arch had been erected. Once he was under the arch he was greeted by the mayor.

Zachary Taylor was impressed by not only the huge crowd and warm welcome, but by that massive arch constructed on his behalf. It was 40-foot wide, 60-foot high. At the very top was a gilded eagle holding in its bill a crown of laurel. Facing the river on the facade of the structure in large gilded letters "Welcome and Buena Vista". Once the ceremonies under the arch were completed, Zachary Taylor was ushered into the Cathedral. When services were completed, he was taken outside where his faithful horse "Old Whitey" was awaiting him.

The second parade was now ready to begin. It was led by an

Triumphant Arch, 1847.

endless line of cavalry followed by equal numbers of infantry. Behind them, on horseback, came Taylor, along with Governor Johnson to his right and Major General Louis on his left. Like the river parade, this one also stretched out a long distance. The crowd that lined the river now lined the parade route. The general was followed by military, fraternal, civic and ethnic groups along with volunteer firemen and scores of others in carriages who participated in the parade.

The evening and official welcome came to an end with an elaborate dinner held at the St. Charles Hotel. As a final tribute to the beloved conquering hero, the Louisiana legislature awarded him a magnificent, ceremonial sword.

It might have been better had he been given the sword when he first arrived. This way it could have helped him cut his way through the crowds as he went from one function to another.

The four mentioned temporary structures were just some of the many built in the square. They may have been temporary in use, but important enough to leave an everlasting impression on those who heard and, in later years, read about them.

NINE O'CLOCK CANNON

As early as 1724, Bienville, then Governor of Louisiana, published the first Black Code. These were regulations to control slaves and at the same time protect them from unsavory masters. One of the 53 articles reference slaves was as follows:

"Who shall not be properly fed, clothed and provided for by their masters may give information thereof to the attorney general of the Superior Council or to any officer of justice of any inferior jurisdiction and may put the written exposition of the wrongs into their hands. Upon which information and even ex. officio should be information come from another quarter, the adjutant general shall prosecute said master without charging any cost to the complainant. It is our royal will that this regulation be observed in all accusations for crimes of barbarous and inhuman treatment brought by slaves against their masters."

This was one of the many articles in the code designed to protect slaves from cruel masters. On the other side of the ledger there were an equal number of articles to control slaves. For example: They were forbidden to carry offensive weapons or sticks and they were not allowed to sell anything. Both of these articles had exceptions—if they carried written permission or wore a badge signifying that they were allowed to do these things.

Slaves were also forbidden from gathering in crowds. Again there were exceptions. On Sundays, dancing in Congo Square was permitted. Slaves were not allowed under any circumstance to roam the streets or countryside after 9:00 p.m. If they were caught after the curfew they were subject to severe punishment.

Each evening in Place d'Armes the quiet of the evening was shattered by the firing of the nine o'clock cannon. This

Nine o'clock cannon.

signified all slaves had to be in their quarters. This nightly ritual was carried out from the square by the all familiar cannon roar from the time the Black Code was activated until 1850 when the square was being completely overhauled. The daily cannon signal and all military parades from that time on were carried out in Congo Square (now called Beauregard Square). The nine o'clock cannon fired its last volley when slavery was abolished on May 11, 1864.

IDEAS — NEVER CAME TO FRUITION

Not everything proposed for the square became a reality. A few 19th century examples:

I'LL DRINK TO THAT

In 1840, some fun-loving soul proposed a bill allowing "Little Cafes" in each corner of the square. Apparently things were not as liberal at that time as they are now, for they didn't drink a toast to success in each corner as they had hoped. The idea simply dried up and the proposer went home thirsty.

STALLS - WERE STALLED

In 1839, thirty fruit merchants were given permission to build stalls in Place d'Armes. Although the license was issued in January, someone, possibly the godfather of the day, made the 30 merchants an offer they couldn't refuse. No record has ever been uncovered that showed fruit stalls ever operated in the square.

YOU WANT TO CLIMB WHERE?

In March, 1839, an unusual request was presented as a form of entertainment. If approved, a certain Signor Sciarra was sure he could make a few bucks. Why not, the idea was novel and had not been done before. He believed, based on other unique forms of entertainment locals enjoyed, that he could not lose. His wife was a gifted tight rope walker, so he applied for and received from the city council permission for his wife to walk a tight rope that would be stretched from the square to the roof of the Cathedral. The city gave its blessing, but stipulated that he would need the blessing of the church. The church apparently said, "You may dance with the devil, but you will never dance your way to the roof of our church." No written record was ever found indicating the event took place.

ONLY ONE ARM AND DEAD —
YET STILL DREW CROWD

There was one incident that did occur that would have been better left undone:

Many slaves through the years escaped their cruel masters. Most were captured, but a few did manage to gain their freedom. A slave named Squire Bras Coupae, meaning "one arm" (because he only had one) escaped. Even though he did not gain lasting freedom, he did give his pursuers a run for their money.

Despite his handicap, he outfoxed any and all who tracked him for a long period of time. His exploits proved to be rather remarkable. Hounds were unable to follow his scent. When they thought they had him cornered, he would vanish like smoke. He eluded every attempt of capture for several years. His exploits were so clever they were spoken about wherever there was a gathering of people. If a mother wished to frighten her child she need only mention Bras Coupae by name. In time his name became known by all.

In the spring of 1837, he was shot and left for dead. Again he outsmarted his captors by playing dead so well that his body was left where he fell. The next day, when they went to collect their trophy, Bras Coupae was nowhere to be found. Finally one Francisco Garcia tracked and killed him, he then brought his body to New Orleans to collect the award. He bragged as to how he skillfully tracked the elusive runaway for close to a week. While Bras Coupae slept one night, he explained, he beat him to death with an iron bar. Mayor Dennis Prier ordered Bras Coupae's body be taken to the square where it was to be exposed to the general public. Morbid curiosity compelled thousands to see what manner of man served as a source of consternation and fear for years.

SQUARE'S TWO GREAT CONTROVERSIES

Once, when they tried to make us see the light, and the other, when they tried to create blight and eliminate sight of the river.

SON et LUMIERE

Son et Lumiere is French for "Sound and Light". Frenchman Pierre Arneud, was the inventor of the sound and light show successfully used at the Parthenon in Athens, the pyramids of Gizah in Egypt, and at Notre Dame de Paris, along with other equally historic places in the world. Arneud arrived in New Orleans in 1965 with the hopes of selling the idea of his highly successful show to the city fathers. Jackson Square was his target as the historic site for the show. Although he was praised on high at Notre Dame, elevated to new heights at Gizah and was on top in Athens, in New Orleans he butted heads with preservationists, felt the sting of the French Quarter resident property owners association and was the benefactor only of lawsuits. After 10 years of frustration and financial drain, Pierre caught a plane. His destination — any place without people who loved their heritage and were willing to sacrifice it for commercial gain. The sounds of success of a cash register were never heard and the lights of his show were short circuited before ever being lit. As one old woman put it, "He can take our girdles and he can take our false teeth, but he will never disrupt our beloved square."

ELEVATED EYE SORE
THAT NEVER GOT OFF THE GROUND

In all the battles to preserve the integrity of the French Quarter and Jackson Square, none were ever more volatile than the fight to derail the proposed elevated roadway that was to run along the riverfront, between the river and the French Quarter/Jackson Square. The odds, like the South's chances in the Civil War were almost nil. In the Civil War the Yankees had the majority of the country's manufacturing facilities and far outnumbered the Confederate States of America in manpower. The Confederate States were mostly agricultural and had to build a military force from scratch. The battle of the elevated expressway was even more lopsided than the odds against the Confederate States of America.

Conditions leading up to the expressway battle, called "The Second Battle of New Orleans" by the newspapers were as follows: In 1956, the federal government began the largest project ever attempted by man. They planned to build 42,500 miles of high speed freeways to connect all cities in the country. The cost was as staggering as the project: $104 billion, with the federal government picking up 90 percent of the cost and states the remaining 10 percent.

Like most major cities in America, New Orleans in the 1960s was suffering from central city traffic congestion. The condition was compounded by people moving to the outer areas of the city or into adjacent smaller towns. A study was made as to what to do to get people to shop downtown instead of one of the ever growing number of shopping centers.

The city pulled out of mothballs an expressway plan done in 1946. With some revisions, and by tying in the federal government plan, this could be the answer to the problem. The idea of an elevated, six-lane, 40-foot-high roadway running between the French Quarter and the river was brought out for all to see. It was like raising a red flag in front of a bull that was already madder than hell.

The city fathers were not really concerned. Why should they be? Behind them was the federal government whose idea it was to build such roadways. Big daddy would surely lead the way against the expected, but paltry opposition. Also behind them was the State Highway Department, the business establishment, and the all-powerful Times-Picayune and States Item newspapers. On the opposition's side were a few minor organizations, including the toothless Louisiana Landmark Society, the Vieux Carré Property Owners Association, and the very small, in comparison to the two big newspapers, Vieux Carré Courier. The two sides, when facing each other, could be compared as follows: Cannons, tanks, phantom jets on one side led by West Point leadership opposing sling shots, chariots and prop driven biplanes led by untrained civilians. The odds may have seemed lopsided, but the elevated roadway opponents had their secret weapon. They were called preservationists, and they proved to be as powerful as the A-bomb. They were led by the "never say die" Mrs. Martha Gilmore Robinson, whose formula for success was desire, dedication and determination, coupled with persistence and a proper attitude. With that formula she was certain that they would be successful in blocking the unwanted, ungodly, sure-to-be-ugly, elevated expressway. To offset the financial disparity the opponents had the Stern family in their camp.

The city was still overconfident, so confident that they built a one-million dollar underground roadway (tunnel) beneath the Rivergate that would be ready when the elevated roadway was completed.

The preservationists went to work, bringing their opponents to court. It was the only battlefield that gave them a chance. They showed that the state and federal highway engineers principal object was to connect two points by the shortest route possible. The plan showed little regard for destruction of historical sites, neighborhoods or the displacement of people. Congress listened to their plans and passed laws that would not allow this to happen.

The city retrenched and decided to propose a near surface level expressway. The proponents did not budge on their stand. The battle raged on for many years, finally ending on July 1, 1969, when U.S. Secretary of Transportation John A. Volte cancelled the proposed Vieux Carré expressway and allocated the funds to another project.

Just as David slew Goliath in the Bible, the giant in the instance of the elevated expressway was slain by the diligent, caring, hardworking preservationists. Their efforts helped preserve the city's most treasured asset, the French Quarter.

There are those who believe to this day that the defeat of the elevated riverfront expressway was not in the best interest of the city's growth and development. On the other hand, the best argument against that belief is a drive down North Claiborne Avenue, where an elevated expressway exists. What was once a beautiful, peaceful, tree-lined street is now a depressing sight, and a good example of urban blight.

Besides preserving the character of the Quarter and the square, there are two other good things that came out of the Second Battle of New Orleans. One: Even when the odds are against you, with the right attitude and right on your side, you can win. And second: The city not only owns an airport, a railroad and a railroad bridge all outside of the city limits, the city now owns a tunnel that cost $1 million in 1960 and has never been used. It has been said tongue-in-cheek that the tunnel does have one use. It raises political mushrooms. That is where they are kept in the dark and are covered with manure.

FOUNTAINS

In Rome, a popular musical score refers to three coins in a fountain. In New Orleans three fountains in a public square were equally popular with the masses for well over half the life of the square.

As was, and still is, the norm in New Orleans, procrastination played its delaying tactics reference the fountains. Noted architect Benjamin Latrobe designed a fountain 40-feet in diameter for Place d'Armes as early as 1819. It was to serve as the square's focal point. The drawings lay idle for many years.

On April 1, 1833, 14 years after the drawings and groundwork had been laid, the state legislature passed an act to incorporate the Commercial Bank of New Orleans. The newly incorporated bank's principal function was to oversee construction of the city's first water works. The ultimate goal was to convey water, using wooden water pipes, from the river, to the water works, and into the houses of the inhabitants. In 1835, the city

council finally got around to voting sufficient funds to build the fountain. It was named the Albert Stein Fountain after the designer of the highly successful waterworks, and a plaque with Stein's name was placed in the base of the fountain. It became instantly popular with the people who watched in amazement as the water reached high into the air where it seemed to dance for a time before falling into the pond. Little children looked at the dancing water, too, but their primary interest was feeding the fish. As popular as the fountain was, its 10 years of existence was a shorter period than the procrastination period getting it built. In 1846 disaster struck. Workmen were putting up a flagpole when a wire broke. The pole crashed onto the fence surrounding the fountain. Although the fountain survived the flagpole accident, it was displaced a short time later. The fountain, in its existence was to have three different homes. On December 4, 1846, it was moved to the fish market and later to the rear of the St. Louis Cathedral.

SECOND FOUNTAIN

The second fountain, although years in coming, was even more popular than the first. Although its overall size and exact location is unknown, the following information is on record:

It was erected in 1895 at a cost of $2,500, and was modeled after the popular illuminated fountain at the Chicago World's Fair. What attracted attention to the fountain was not only its dancing water, but the fact that it was multicolored. A motor in the base rotated a series of colored glass disks through which a small searchlight passed, giving the jets of water the appearance of color. For many years the motion, sound and color spectacle drew large crowds every night of the week.

THIRD FOUNTAIN

On April 29, 1960, French President General Charles De Gaulle paid a visit to New Orleans. A short distance inside the Chartres Street entrance to the square, De Gaulle addressed the crowd. That same year a fountain to commemorate his visit was erected on the exact spot where he delivered his speech.

Little did he realize the importance of that occasion. Where else would Ruthie the Duck Lady bring her duck to swim had the fountain not been built?

Ruthie the Duck Lady

Ruthie the Duck Lady

STATUES

In 1840, Andrew Jackson, savior of the city and past president of the United States, paid his third and final visit to New Orleans. He was invited by a group of grateful citizens to attend the ceremony celebrating the 25th anniversary of the Battle of New Orleans. From the moment he stepped off the deck of the steamer Vicksburg, he was treated with the attention one would expect for such an important man. As he had done days prior to the January 8, 1815 battle, he once again reviewed troops in the public square 25 years after the famous battle was won. On January 13th, one more trip to the square was scheduled. This time the occasion was the laying of a cornerstone for a proposed monument to be constructed in his honor. The cornerstone he laid, for unknown reasons, was not in the center of the square, but left of the exact center. Fifteen years later when the Jackson Monument Association was advised the statue was nearing completion, it was agreed the monument should be moved to the exact center of the square. The decision was also made to remove the cornerstone laid by Jackson and place it in the granite base of the pedestal that would support the statue.

On October 30, 1855, association members removed the cornerstone from where it was laid by Jackson. The daily Picayune recorded what had transpired: "The workmen commenced a little after daybreak . . . and did not reach the box until 11 o'clock, so firmly had it been set originally. They first came to a square of granite on which was inscribed '8th January, 1815' and beneath this was a granite block, hollow in the center, which contained the copper box . . . This was imbedded in a mass of bricks and cement which had become as hard as the granite itself. After getting this out of the ground, the lower block was carefully removed with its contents and reverently deposited in the center of the pedestal, and the covering placed upon it."

Word spread quickly throughout the city about the copper box Andrew Jackson placed in the cornerstone. A huge crowd soon surrounded the area and wanted to know—others demanded to know—what the box contained. The committee flatly refused to reveal what was in the box. Instead of yielding to the demand of the crowd, a cavity was made in the pedestal brick-work large enough to hold not only the Jackson copper box, but a second box containing numerous items collected by the committee. Among the items was a transcript of the January 11, 1851 meeting which was the association's first. Coins in the box included 1855 $3 and $1 gold pieces and a 3 cent piece. A lengthy list of items placed in the box by the association is on record. What the Jackson copper box contained remains a mystery.

THE STATUE DEDICATION

The Andrew Jackson statue commissioned to be built by Clark Mills was not dedicated on the 40th anniversary of the Battle of New Orleans as planned. It was dedicated on February 9, 1856. The delay was caused by a shipping problem.

Andrew Jackson

The committee, having fulfilled its dream of the dedication of a statue of Andrew Jackson, put the final touch on the ceremony spiritually—not the religious, but the liquid kind. Once the formal ceremonies were completed, six bottles of Pony brandy costing $12 were shared by the committee members. The purchase of the brandy had been approved by Mayor C.M. Waterman.

OUT OF SIGHT
OUT OF MIND

Although the statue of Andrew Jackson is the most photographed and talked and written about statue in New Orleans, it is not the city's oldest. That distinction belongs to four statues located in the four corners of the square. Even though changing seasons is not one of those things enjoyed by locals, the statues represent the four seasons — autumn, summer, winter and spring. They predate Jackson's statue by four years. The city purchased the four statues from d'Lanta for $100 each. Marble bases and installation brought the cost to $1,030 or $257.57 each. What a bargain! It has cost the city only $1.84 per year per statue.

WHO IS HE?

Andrew Jackson's head

As popular as the Andrew Jackson statue is, if you were to show the drawing of the head on this page to the thousands who see it each week, chances are very few would identify it as the head of Andrew Jackson. The picture is of a plaster cast made from the original. It is in a sense a form of insurance because of the following incident:

On February 22, 1934, a young prankster climbed the statue and pulled the pin holding the head to the body, decapitating Jackson. Luckily a museum employee found the head on the ground the next day and took it to the Cabildo for safe keeping. Before the head was put back, a plaster cast was made and put on display in the museum.

Note: Through the years Andy not only lost his head, but his hat and saber on numerous occasions. The only part missing at this time is the spur on his right boot. With the city budget being what it is, Jackson has little chance of getting a new spur. But then, he's not going anywhere. Although the statue, even under close scrutiny, seems to be made of one solid piece, it is comprised of over sixty parts.

SECRET VAULT IN BASE OF JACKSON MONUMENT?

In 1869, 13 years after the dedication of the statue of Andrew Jackson, a story appeared in the Picayune newspaper that captured the imagination, attention and deep interest of its readers. According to the story, two men met at the base of the statue as they had done previously on numerous occasions. One of them noticed for the first time a small iron pin sticking out of one of the granite blocks. Perhaps the light on that particular day was perfect for them to notice the pin. One of the men, using the point of his walking cane, pushed the pin. Both men

Secret door?

were startled, even shocked when a well concealed door, looking just like the stone base, opened. The men cautiously looked into the five-foot by five-foot chamber. It was stuffed with gold bars, silver coins, and many chests filled with diamonds, emeralds and other precious stones. What a fabulous find they had made! Their thoughts then turned to where the cache might have come from. Their guesses ranged from pirate booty to treasures stored there by some foreign prince or king about to be dethroned by opposing forces.

The answer to the question was in the newspaper. All the reader needed to do was look at the top of the page, the date was April 1. This was another of the famous April fool's jokes played on its readers by the Picayune newspaper.

LIKE A GOOD WINE
JACKSON SQUARE GETS BETTER WITH AGE

The uses of the Square presently are a far cry from the early days. Early on, the square was used for punishment of criminals, including highly attended public hangings. Today, it no longer draws people for hangings, but hang around the square they do for sheer pleasure. At one time, burning at the stake was carried out. Now, the only burning is sunburn suffered while attending the largest jazz brunch in the world during the French Quarter Festival and other equally enjoyable events. The loud noise of the nine o'clock cannon was evident in the early years. Now, the place is a panorama of sound. From the laughter of children at play to a jazz concert on a lazy Sunday afternoon, or the narration of a tour guide with a group following like baby ducks behind their mother straining to hear every word the guide utters.

In the early years, the area was not very pleasant to the eye. For many years there weren't even trees or grass to add color. Little by little, improvements were made. Shade trees were planted and in time gave shade. Next came flowers, shrubs and walkways. As the appearance improved, benches were added along with fountains and statues. Even though it was used from the beginning, the more functional and appealing it became, the more popular it became.

The face of the Square changed dramatically and constantly during the 19th century, when temporary structures were built for various celebrations.

The Square has become increasingly popular during the 20th century. For one thing, locals' visits there have been exceeded by the numbers of conventioneers and tourists who come from all corners of the world to visit the city. For another, the Square has become the focal point of fun events, including the Spring Fiesta, French Quarter Festival, Christmas carolling, weekend concerts during the summer, etc.

Not everything planned or proposed for the Square became

a reality, but those things that did, made her as functional and pleasing to the eye as humanly possible. If there is a place that could be classified as heaven on earth, the Square would have to be one of the names submitted. If I were one of the judges I would cast my vote for Jackson Square, for she is not only the most historic square of ground in Louisiana, but one of the most picturesque as well.

To get a true feeling of Jackson Square, might I suggest the following. One early morning, in the middle of April or October, the city's most pleasant months in terms of weather, go by yourself or with a friend who promises not to break the silence and just quietly sit on one of the benches facing the Cathedral. As the sun rises and the city awakes you will get a feeling of the heartbeat and pulse of the community starting off slowly and building up steadily as the day goes on. You will hear the church bells ring every fifteen minutes, as they have done for centuries. The doors of the church tend to squeak when they open for the early arrivals who shuffle down the banquette and enter the old venerable church. Here they begin their day in prayer and thanksgiving to their God. People in all modes of dress begin to move. Bartenders and waiters in tuxedos who have worked all night are going in one direction, and in the opposite, shopkeepers who are just beginning their day. You will see patrons who have been at the bars all night figuratively, as well as literally, staggering along. Some know, and others not, where they are going. Hurrying along comes an old lady with her prayer cap and purse, followed by her husband dressed in suit and tie. She fusses saying he has made them late for mass. He softly replies he would never dream of going to mass without coat and tie any more than anyone would pay a visit to any other king or person of nobility without being properly attired. It was she who misplaced his tie, he mumbles, not him. The morning will also bring children in uniforms, all on their way to the grade school in the Quarter. Without exception they will all bid you the time of day. Once the retail stores on the bottom floors of the Pontalba apartments open, shoppers begin arriving. Some go to have a cup of coffee to help start their day. Others have a full breakfast; no one should ever shop on an empty stomach. Vendors by the scores are next. They deliver bread, milk, beer, wine, linens and merchandise of every description to the coffee shop, retail clothing, jewelry or possibly the kite shop. As the day wears on, one by one, the horse and buggies begin lining up outside the square. The drivers congregate to talk, drink coffee or smoke a cigarette to help prepare them to face the day, and catch up on the gossip of the previous day. Once the working day begins, the traffic noises increase. Between the screeching of brakes you will hear a car, or a bus horn followed by sounds so loud that it drowns out all other noises. For a moment you cannot even hear yourself breathe. When you turn around, you realize it is the horn of a 600 foot ocean going vessel passing only several hundred feet from where you are sitting. If you thought the volume of noise was attention-getting, your attention will really be focused when you realize that you are looking up, way up, as the ship glides by. The sight serves as a reminder that the city is below sea level. The ships, tugboats, barges and all of the river traffic that pass in front of the square are higher than the square itself. The steamboat Natchez loaded with vacationers pulls away from the dock as the calliope plays "Dixie". Intermingled with all the noises will be a jazz band, or simply a single musician vying for the attention of tourists' dollars. Not far away is a magician pulling rabbits out of a hat in hopes that he will get the tourists to pull dollars out of their pockets and purses. If you are lucky, you will be there on the day that Ruthie The Duck Lady comes by to take her duck for a swim in the General De Gaulle Fountain. You will hear birds singing, pigeons cooing and sometimes even one of the ladies of the evening who stays to the side of the Square to woo potential customers as they pass. The hum of a lawn mower, the rap of a hammer working on the reconstruction of the Cabildo, the scraping sound of a shovel of the street cleaners plying their trade, the ring of the ice cream man's bell to attract your attention, and even though he doesn't make a sound you will know the Lucky Dog hot dog man is in the vicinity because of the aroma that permeates from his cart.

Yes, happiness is found in the simple things of life. The ultimate happiness for me would be to sit quietly in Jackson Square in the shade of a tree, reading a good book and eating a muffuletta sandwich washed down by a good old Barq's root beer while a jazz band plays softly in the background. Now that's what you call living New Orleans style.

Happiness is . . .

Art Credits: Photography and Drawings

References are to page numbers:

Buddy Stall: 17, 22, 24, 33, 47, 58, 75, 76, 81, 85, 101, 104, 107, 108, 110, 123, 178, 198, 199, 200, 209, 222, 237, 241, 246, 278, 287, 288

Lane Casteix: 18, 37, 38, 39, 43, 44, 52, 54, 56, 60, 62, 64, 67, 73, 74, 77, 79, 82, 87, 90, 98, 103, 113, 122, 125, 127, 128, 131, 136, 139, 140, 142, 152, 156, 157, 177, 180, 181, 183, 185, 187, 189, 192, 196, 197, 201, 202, 205, 206, 207, 215, 223, 224, 225, 226, 228, 229, 230, 235, 238, 239, 242, 244, 247, 252, 253, 254, 264, 268, 269, 272, 273, 276, 285, 290, 292, 293

Yvette Ponthier: 59, 68, 92, 105, 120, 211, 297

Wade Ponthier: 194, 202, 203

Archdiocese of New Orleans: 41, 65, 119, 138, 144, 159, 160, 161, 162, 163, 164, 165, 166, 167, 168, 169, 170, 171, 278

Tulane University, University Archives, Howard-Tilton Memorial Library, New Orleans, Louisiana: 49

U.S. Custom House: 96

Louisiana State Museum: 111, 257, 276

David Noll: 233, 236

Henri Gondolfo: 256